I0781723

90 DAYS TO SUCCESS: MINDSET

From Survival & Stress to Thriving in Awesomeness

A Mindset Reset Warrior's Guide for
Transformational Change

Written By

Helen Walton

Helen Walton asserts the moral right to be identified as the author of this work.

Copyright © 2024 Helen Walton

ISBN: 9798332039201

Originally published in Australia 2024

Imprint: Independently published

All rights reserved. No parts of this book may be copied, reproduced or transmitted in any form or by any electronic or mechanical means, including photocopying, recoding or by any information storage and retrieval system, without the written permission of the author/publisher except where permitted by law. For more information, contact the author/publisher at www.mindsetresetwarriors.com

10 9 8 7 6 5 4 3 2 1

This book is first and foremost dedicated to my kids. The little pieces of my heart that broke free from me to form new life and create a reason for me to go on, to live, to be the best version of me I can be. Without them I would not be the person I am today; I would not be thriving, succeeding, shooting for the stars and living my best life. Without them I shudder to think where I would be. I might not even be here at all.

Secondly, I devote this book to you, Mindset Reset Warrior. I devote it to every person reading this book because if you are here, it means you are taking the steps needed to break free from the chains of your own mind and build your best life. To heal, to grow and to make the best of this finite existence you have here on this earth and that is a beautiful thing. That is hard. It takes courage and strength and awareness. I'm proud of you, I love you and I support you. Now get reading this book and set your shiny soul free so you too can then go on to shine a light for others to thrive and succeed in their lives.

Let's do this!

Contents

A Quick Backstory About the Author

Did you ever feel you were meant for great things, have big dreams and a million ideas about who you wanted to be? I did. I wanted to be a writer, teacher, business owner, mother, and, most of all, help the world. I always knew I would. Despite a rocky start to life, causing people to tell me I was no good and would never amount to anything, I just knew I would be great!

My name is Helen, I am 34 years young and yes, I am doing great! I am a mother to three big-hearted, brilliant kids, an educator passionate about supporting high-needs children, a writer, a psychology degree student, and a small business owner going on ten years. Here I am doing not just one of the things I dreamed of doing but ALL of them and more! Was it luck or privilege? Did I meet someone who got me on a path to success? No. It was hard work, determination, and an unwavering belief that I could make it. It all came from a burning desire to be happy, content and make the most of life by living it the way I wanted to live it. For me.

For a long time, I was depressed and suffered anxiety. I had been through a lot of experiences in my younger years that left me with scars, broken pieces and shitload of trauma. Although underneath I still had that belief I was destined for great things and could do anything I set my mind to, as the years went on, that burning flame was dimming. Life and all its challenges was smothering out my light a little more each year, and the voices of self-doubt, self-criticism and self-hate were getting louder, drowning out the inner voice of that child with big dreams. My life was like one big shit-show drama/horror serries written by drunken monkeys and I could go into details about everything I've been through, but you might mistake this book for a poorly written and somewhat unbelievable fiction story. Life really got that crazy-topsy-turvy for me.

Eventually at the beginning of 2023, after a string of events tipped the scale on the build-up of trauma, depression, stress, and struggle, I had a physical and mental breakdown which ultimately led to the most profound and incredible transformation. My life changed entirely and finally; I was on the path I needed to be on. I finally started to learn how to heal from the abuse and mental health struggles I'd been suffering through most of my life and redirected my mind and entire life trajectory.

Now here I am. Thriving with a positive mindset, living every day with so much love, flow and contentment. I still feel human emotions like frustration and sadness because that is perfectly normal, but I am no longer controlled by them, and they visit me rather infrequently and only in small bouts. It is such an amazing feeling to live this way after struggling and suffering for so long. I never thought that pain would stop and now I can't even see me feeling that way ever again. Not now that I've learned how to be in control of my emotions, my mind and my entire life. The best part about it all is not only have I finally learned how to love myself and love my life, but I have also become an even better role model for my amazing children and am living the life I want. I get to live my life on my terms doing the things I love and making a difference to the lives of others along the way.

Throughout my career in education, I have always been a passionate advocator for support for high needs and at-risk kids, focusing not just on their education but their mental health and need for acceptance and care as an entire human being. However, I came to a profound realisation: the most significant impact I can make is not just through the children in my role in the education setting, but by empowering their parents, caregivers, and every adult grappling with unhealed trauma and mindset challenges. For at the root of all issues kids face there are adults guiding the way for them. When those adults are struggling and in need of support, whether through challenges they face now or because of their own childhood struggles, they are not at their best to set an example for the children of tomorrow.

I strongly believe that by supporting adults to heal from their own struggles and trauma, we can create a ripple effect that transforms the lives of children and, ultimately, the world. My mission is to equip adults with the tools they need to overcome their struggles, fostering a healthier, more positive environment for the next generation. With a heart full of compassion and love and a mind brimming with knowledge and experience in multiple areas, I am committed to paving the way for a brighter, more hopeful future for all. So, thanks for being here and doing your part to make the world a better place by making yourself a better person. Because that is truly how we transform the world; through one healed soul at a time.

Introduction

Welcome to the Mindset Reset Warriors' guide to reset your mindset in 90 days. This instructional book is designed to guide you through a transformative journey of resetting your mindset for positive change. While the journey to change can be a long, hard road, full of challenges, roadblocks and invisible mind-battles with brain gremlins, it is possible to significantly shift your way of thinking in as little as 90 days or much less. In doing so, you pave the way for ongoing change and success by establishing and strengthening this new positive way of seeing yourself and the world around you.

Our mindset shapes how we perceive the world, approach challenges, navigate life's ups and downs and how we see ourselves. Your own self-image, beliefs and inner dialogue are the core foundation of your mindset, and your mindset is the core foundation of you. So, who do you want to be at your core? If you're here reading this book then it's probably because you've reached a pivotal time in your life where you're fed up with feeling like you've been run down repeated by semi-trailers loaded with manure; you've decided you no longer want to wrestle with the Negative Nelly's taking up space in your precious mind and are ready to blast your past clean off the radar of your focus so you can turn your view towards a brighter, easier future. Chances are you know you're capable of so much more but are feeling as stuck and depressed as a certain horse in a certain childhood movie sinking into a mire of despair (if you know you know and you're probably still broken inside from this scene that is on "never-ending" repeat in your memories). So, if you're ready to do the work then there are a few things you need to know first.

I wonder if you know that research has shown that by age 35, 95% of your mindset is pre-programmed with thoughts and beliefs based on your past experiences. That's why some people are a train-wreck, some people are the train conductor, some are the nonchalant passengers, and some are the crazy person in the back car screaming about intelligent killer ice-creams taking over the world and making everyone uncomfortable. Depending on your experiences you will have different beliefs, habits, thoughts and behaviours pre-programed into you. Your subconscious mind is more powerful than you realise because your brain is a phenomenal tool that takes in everything around you, whether you realise it or not, and it has been since the day you were born. The renowned ancient philosopher Aristotle once said, "Give me a child until age seven, and I will show you the man." Even then, there was an understanding that a child is conditioned to be a certain way based on their environment in the first years of life.

For the first seven or eight years, children are highly susceptible to absorbing whatever information is thrown at them, either directly or indirectly. They learn from how their caregivers act, what they observe, and what they are told. During this time, the brain develops rapidly, and by age twelve, a child's brain becomes more analytical. This is around the age they start thinking for themselves. It is a delicate time in development as they are also going through many other changes. The mindset is now being shaped by a great deal more external factors. It's not just about what their small circle in their immediate environment is showing them; it's what's coming from observing their friends and others, what the kids at school are saying, what their teachers say, what the television programs (and these days angry social media cats in bow ties) are saying. They are starting to form an even broader concept of who they are and what the world around them is like, developing a mindset based on factors that are still out of their control.

Now, while the early years are the most important for cognitive development, and adolescence plays a significant role in the ongoing social development of an individual, the brain goes on growing and developing until a person is in their mid-twenties to early thirties and thus comes the figures that show by age 35 you have already been pre-programed to be you. But it still doesn't stop there. Due to the brain's remarkable ability to constantly learn new things through the beauty of neuroplasticity, it can be rewired, re-programed and create new neurological connections to help a person develop and learn new skills right up until the day it stops functioning (aka, until you die or suffer some horrific brain injury).

This incredible ability can be harnessed for good, but it can also be utilised negatively, which is usually unintentional and subconscious. For example, traumatic situations you encounter as an adult affect your neurology and biology. Addictions and other bad habits begin to shape how you feel about yourself and see yourself. Unhealthy relationships, abuse and hostile treatment from others, working too hard in a job you hate, stress, financial troubles, and so many more things are still shaping you. Additionally, living in a state of stress and survival is not only impacting your mindset and mental health, but the chemicals also flooding through your body that come with these negative emotions are damaging your physical wellbeing as well. That is why it is essential to start taking steps to care for your mental and emotional wellbeing NOW.

But there is hope for you OB1-K-Not-Copywrite. You can use the force – I mean, the power – within you to rewire your thoughts and redirect your life in whatever way you decide. No matter how far you've walked on one path through life there are always turns to take to guide you to a better road. It takes time and consistent, intentional action but no matter what you have been through, research shows us you have the ability within your incredible mind to rewire your brain and completely change your life. Your current mindset is based on your past and may not benefit your ideal future because we humans tend to live in a loop (let's call it Groundhog Day).

Your mindset decides how you think, and how you think governs how you feel, how you think and feel determines how you act and show up for yourself in your current life, and how you act creates your current life circumstances. This is all shaping your personality, your personal reality and guiding your future. Therefore, unless we make a conscious decision not to, we are constantly living in a subconscious loop of the past. When you reach the end of this equation, you can see that your current life circumstances make you think and feel a certain way. You begin to realise the negative and detrimental loop you are stuck in, starting with your mindset. Change your mindset, and you will change your entire life. Change how you think, and you will no longer be stuck in a loop of the old you but will always be moving forward on a path of greatness, contentment, and growth.

Are you having an aha moment yet? Got a little metaphorical light bulb hovering about your beautiful head like you're in your own cartoon skit? If not yet, then but the time we're through here you will. You will start to see the pieces clicking into place because, throughout this book, we will delve deeply into the intricacies of our extraordinary minds and lives and uncover why we think and feel the way we do. We will explore techniques, exercises, and strategies to help you overcome limiting beliefs, adopt a growth-oriented mindset, karate chop brain gremlins, and cultivate a more empowered and fulfilling life. We will dive deep into you and, simultaneously, learn how to step outside of you to get to the root of what's holding you back from true change and see where you need to concentrate your energy to rewire your thinking.

This is not wishful thinking, fairy tale lore, or hopes and dreams. The knowledge and action steps you're about to explore in the pages of this epic mindset reset guide are based on researched-backed information and strategies grounded in psychology and proven to work for anyone, even those who have come from the worst lives and have suffered what seems like insurmountable challenges. So, let's jump in right now, uncover who you really are, and get you underway to becoming the person you were always meant to be.

How to get the most out of this guide

I wrote this guide as the first book in my 90 Days to Success series because mindset is the foundation to having a successful life in any way, shape, or form. It doesn't matter what success looks like to you; whether it's wealth, a type of career, a healthy, happy family, a content, simple life or whatever it is you want to be and achieve, mindset it the core of it all. You could win the lotto and be set for life, run a multi-million-dollar company, be rich and famous, have your dream house and dream job, and have an amazing partner, but if your mindset isn't serving you, you will never be whole and know how to live in flow and contentment. People with unhealthy mindsets never have enough no matter what material things they acquire or goals they succeed at accomplishing. They always think they need more before they can finally be happy. But they have it backwards. You don't need succuss and accomplishment to be happy, you need to find joy in the ordinary and gratitude in what you already have. Once you can do that, the power that kind of peace evokes propels you with such force you can achieve so much more than you could before.

As mindset is vital to living a life where you feel whole and happy, with success and abundance in any form and capacity, I want to ensure you get the absolute most out of this book and the information within. That is why the books in this series are written to be short, concise, and actionable. In other words, short and sweet with minimal bullshit and maximum impact. You can read or listen to them in around an hour or two, and they are written in a way that you can absorb and understand the information needed to help you transform your life in impactful ways. I also through it a little of my quirky personality so you don't fall asleep or get distracted. Like the advertising says, it's not your ordinary snooze-fest self-help book.

Plus, not only is this information based on decades (or even centuries) of scientifically proven research and psychological knowledge, but everything in these guides has also been tried and tested by me. I am sharing things that have helped me transform my life completely. Through decades of trauma, struggle, addictions, bad habits, ADHD, depression, anxiety, and even physical health struggles, I – a busy mum/student/business owner/educator – was able to heal and transform my entire life with the information I am sharing in these books. No mean feat I tell you and something I never thought was possible for me, but with the right knowledge and tools it was not only possible to shift my mindset for success but it became something second nature to me.

Upon purchasing this book, I recommend you take some time to read or listen to it all the way through in one sitting by listening to 25 minutes at a time and taking 5-minute breaks in between each interval. This is called the Pomodoro technique and is a proven method for keeping your mind focused on the information at hand as it more effectively lets information sink it. This way, you can absorb all the information without getting distracted or off track. If you're telling yourself you're so busy and don't have an hour, STOP that nonsense right now!! That right there is one of your limiting beliefs in action, and it is a lie you are telling yourself. You do have an hour in your day for you and for transformational change because you are worth the time it takes to learn to live your best life. Your life is yours. Your time is yours. You own it, and you control is, so start taking control now by establishing one hour in whatever way you can and read or listen to this book. You may even want to listen to it while you go on auto-piolet to clean your house or commute to work if you have a long drive there and back.

Once you have read/listened once, it's time to listen again, but this time you are taking action. Make sure you have a journal, exercise book, blank word document or the free PDF workbook that goes with this guide, which you can download here. Now read/listen to each section of the book, following along with the PDF and context of the guide to take action in rewiring your mindset and reshaping your life. Research shows that by writing things down and repeating them, the information solidifies in your brain quicker and easier (especially if you manually write by hand). But hold your horses hot-shot, you're not done. After two weeks, listen to/read the book again, then once more after one month, then two months. Then, after 90 days, read/listen to it in full again and this time you will be reflecting on how far you've come and areas of focus to work on next. Remember, repetition is crucial in solidifying new information and hardwiring new synaptic connections in your brain (which is why you might notice I repeat certain key information throughout the book, as these things are extremely important and need to sink in).

Read/listen to this book repeatedly; as you do, recognise how far you have come and how you have transformed your life and continue to look at how you think and feel daily. While it is possible to significantly shift your mindset to a new, more positive outlook in such a short time, maintaining that state of being is an ongoing journey that takes dedication and an inherent awareness of yourself and your mind. It is easy to fall back to old habits, patterns, and negative ways of thinking when that has been our default normal for so long. Commit to yourself and your journey to a better life. Use this guide as your stepping stone and catapult your way to a more positive mindset then, whenever you feel yourself slipping, listen to it again and keep your mindset focused on the continual journey to success. Reinforce with yourself how taking the time and energy to transform your life now is setting you up for a more powerful, peaceful and intentional future.

"You cannot solve a problem with the same mind that created it."

~ Albert Einstein

"You will achieve nothing in this world without courage."

~ Aristotle

"When the student is ready, the teacher appears."

~ Lao Tzu

PART ONE

Mindset Checkpoint: Are you thriving or just surviving?

Let's dive right in. If this is your second time reading/listening to the book and you're ready to take notes and take action, be sure to have your journal or PDF print out ready to go for Step 1 because it's full steam ahead from here. To begin you are going to assess your current mindset. Assessing your mindset involves a deliberate examination of the thoughts, beliefs, and attitudes that shape your perception of yourself and your environment. The way you think influences the way you feel and act in any situation, so it is essential to understand your thoughts and beliefs, where they came from, why you have them and decide whether they are the truth or a lie you've been subconsciously telling yourself. Only by becoming conscious of your unconscious thoughts, feelings and behaviours can you begin to do the work to illicit true and meaningful change in your life.

This process often begins with introspection, where you take time to reflect on your thought patterns, emotional responses, and underlying beliefs about yourself and the world at large. You can gain insight into your mindset and its impact on your behaviour and well-being through practices such as mindfulness, meditation, journaling, therapy, seeking feedback from others and patting random dogs – ok maybe not that last one, technically speaking, but it's fun to do and definitely cathartic. In exploring your mindset, you can uncover both empowering and limiting beliefs, identify areas for growth, and cultivate a greater sense of self-awareness.

All these things will be addressed further throughout the book but for now we will begin with just a basic look at who you are and what you want to change. Understanding your mindset is essential for personal growth and development because your mindset, choices and actions are the main things holding you back from reaching your full potential and living the life you want to live. Sometimes your mindset is the *only* thing holding you back. You have full control over your mindset which means you have control over your life. While you may not always have control over your external world in every sense, you do have control over how you react to adverse situations. The peace and authority you gain with this control is only possible with a strong, healthy mindset.

Understanding your mindset is vital for enhancing your ability to navigate challenges, cope with setbacks, and foster resilience in the face of adversity. Having a negative mindset versus a positive one is the difference between:

- Having a victim mentality or an opportunistic mentality.
- Being rushed and stressed all the time or having calm, peaceful mornings, and days.
- Ruminating on things that ruin your whole day, week, month or longer or calmly and healthily redirecting negative emotions in an appropriate timeframe.
- Feeling lost, broken, in lack and at war with yourself and the world around you or feeling purpose, joy, abundance, and peace.

What do you want to feel? Who do you want to be? How do you want your days and weeks and life to flow and unfold? How many pet dragons do you want to own? These are the questions you need to ask yourself and answer in truth to see that if you are not living the life you want to live, you need to take action to change now. Not when you get a better job or better partner. Not when the kids are older and easier (spoiler alert: parenting doesn't get easier it just changes). Not when, when, when, when the sky turns purple, and the trees grow leaves-down roots-up. NOW! Right here, right now, with this amazing book today. I am here guiding you, showing you how through research and experience (both personal and professional). I am cheering you on and know you can do this because I have done it myself and seen countless others following the same advice completely transform their life and some from the most difficult situations. You've got this. Let's go.

Step one: We start assessing our current mindset by reflecting on our beliefs, attitudes, and thought patterns related to various aspects of life, such as success, relationships, challenges, and self-worth. If you are using the PDF there are some statements for you to evaluate that will help you see whether you have a more negative mindset or tend to be more on the positive side (if you're here reading this book seeking guidance, we're going to assume it's more negative but fill that out anyway).

You will answer and score each one as follows: 0=always, 1=often, 2=sometimes, 3=barely ever, or 4=never. If you are not using the PDF printout prepare your book by putting the title: "My current mindset score" at the top of the page and I will list the statements here. For each one, you will write down your answer based on the options just given. For example, if the answer to your question is never you will write down the number 4. I suggest that you don't just write down the answers in your book but write down the full statement and then your score. That way, when you come back to reflect you can see exactly what you were scoring and assessing yourself on because at the end of the one month and again at two months and three months, you will be doing the same assessment to see how things have changed. Please be honest with yourself. No one ever has to see this worksheet if you don't want them to. This is about being honest and aware of your thoughts and feelings to understand what you need to focus on the most for intentional change. So, with that in mind, let's have a look at your current mindset.

1. When something goes wrong, one of the first things I think is something like, "oh that's about right," "so what else is new," "bad stuff always happens to me," "I'm not surprised," or "why does stuff like this always happen to me?"

2. Mornings are hard because I'm often rushed and worrying about what I must do for the day, or I'm focused on bad things that have happened or will happen.

3. I often dwell on past mistakes or failures and feel guilty and ashamed for not doing/achieving the things I want to or say I will.

4. I worry about things beyond my control like local/world events, other people's behaviours, thoughts, and feelings (i.e. if they like me or how they treat me) or other people's lives and problems in general.

5. I spend more time focusing on what is wrong rather than what is right and what I don't have rather than what I do have.

6. When something doesn't go to plan or happens out of order (plans cancelled, late for work, cut off in traffic etc) I get easily frustrated or upset and then dwell on the issue for a prolonged time.

7. I doubt my ability to do a lot of different things, to change and to cope with problems.

8. I worry about the future and believe I will always have a hard life.

9. I think about all the bad things I've been through in the past, letting it affect me now in my everyday life.

10. I feel discouraged by setbacks and struggle to stay on track with the goals I've set because I don't have a lot of belief in myself.

Now let's add up the total of your answers. A total of 0-17 is an extremely negative mindset, 18-25 is rather negative, 26-33 is somewhat positive and 34-40 is very positive. Once you have a total, put your score with its rating (i.e. 14 = extremely negative mindset) underneath and take a moment to reflect on what you've written down. It is now crucial to pause here and go inward. Remember what was discussed at the beginning of this book and solidify it in your mind: your mindset right now is not you. Your current mindset is a result of your past and present external situations and environments that have shaped you. You do have the neurological power to rewire your brain to think differently which in turn will make you feel and act differently.

You may have heard the saying neurons (or nerve cells) that fire together wire together. If not, basically what this means is that the miraculous little neurons your brain is made of work with one another to create new connections and solidify new learning through linking and repeating action. So, this means that no matter what thoughts your mind is enacting within you and no matter what behaviours you are exhibiting that are reinforcing your beliefs in these negative thoughts, you *can* change. Now that you are taking the steps to recognise the need for change you can start to take action. Now that you are coming to be aware of who you are and how you think, you can enforce new approaches to changing old ways even if you've failed to do so before. Rome wasn't build in a day and neither was your current mindset so be prepared to give time and patience to your mindset reset journey.

There is something else that is fundamental in exhibiting the ability to change your mindset and therefore change your life. That is the unwavering feeling inside you that you *need* to do this. If you constantly let your feelings outweigh your thoughts, you will not change because it is your thoughts that control your feelings. That might sound a little confusing so let's go back to what we discussed earlier. That loop of thoughts creates feelings that determine your actions which shapes your circumstances impacting how you think and feel. Now understand that your brain is constantly working in the background to solidify habits and behaviours to the point where they are subconscious and automatic because it means a lot less work for the brain and body. If you don't have to think about doing something and you just do it, that's what your brain wants. Therefore, all your current thoughts and beliefs are already solidified in your brain as a habitual way of thinking. It is so automatic and subconscious that your body already knows how to feel about certain things, people, and situations without you even having to think about it and in that instance, sometimes the feeling comes before the thought.

Let me explain that further with a little example. Your current mindset is that people don't like you and they are often talking about you behind your back. That kind of belief makes you feel uncomfortable, sad, resentful, or irritable. Now you walk into the lunchroom at work or show up to a family event and even though your mind isn't consciously thinking "oh everyone in here hates me and will talk about me as soon as I leave," your body already knows how to feel in this situation. It's ready to do its job and its primal purpose is to protect you from harm and uncomfortable situations. That means, subconsciously and automatically it recognises this situation from repeated exposure to it with your negative mindset and sends your body into anxiety, stress, depression, or frustration.

To rewire this, you need to consciously try to overrule that feeling. Make a conscious effort to stop, recognise it and tell yourself it is not real, and it is not who you are. You need to convince yourself that most people aren't thinking about you at all because they've got their own problems and even if the people you're associating with don't like you, then what you're overcoming is the uncomfortable feeling that goes with that. Your self-worth isn't determined by another person's opinion of you. Remember though, you can't make this override work by doing it once or twice. You need to do it repeatedly until you overwrite the old programming and solidify the new belief that elicits joy and comfort, rather than stress and anxiety. Oftentimes, people try to change negative thought patterns and overrule detrimental beliefs with affirmations and positive thinking but when it doesn't work at first, they go straight back to the old belief they are incapable of change because they still feel the way they used to. The problem here is not giving yourself the time, patience, and practice to establish the new ways of thinking and letting the new thoughts gain enough strength to override the old ones.

Here's one more important thing to understand about your brain. Without going into technical terms and losing you with the labels of the parts of the brain – as much as I do love words that just roll off the tongue like amygdala and prefrontal cortex – I'll explain this as simple as possible. You have a primal part of your brain that is automatic, and its job is to protect you from harm and things that are uncomfortable and don't "feel" right. Then you have the executive function part that makes you do the things you want and need to do regardless of how they feel. That part is not automated and takes conscious effort to activate. This is why it is so hard to make and break habits in the beginning. Your primal, pleasure-seeking, protective part goes "um yeah no thanks that's not fun or nice or comfortable so let's avoid that," and kicks into action all on its own, with no hassle at all and no thought or effort from you. While the part you need to exert the effort and take the action is just sitting there waiting for you to force it to override the primal brain. The thing is, that part doesn't work so well when the primal brain is already launching into action with its anxiety, stress, anger, sadness, and other powerful protective emotions.

Now, as much as I love all the scientific-technical content I've learned in the fields of psychology and neuroscience, this guide is not meant to be too in-depth, so I won't fluff it full of all that stuff. However, it is still important that you understand how your brain works to a certain extent to get a better chance at making the changes you need. Once you realise that you are essentially being automatically steered to do what your brain thinks is protecting you, you can let go of telling yourself you're useless, lazy, too damaged, incapable of change, not smart enough to domesticate a crocodile and all those other limiting beliefs that are stopping you from pushing through that tough spot at the beginning of your journey.

So many people hold the mantra "I am what I am", or "this is just the way I am, and I can't change", but it is simply not true. You may be the way you are right now because of all the things you've been through, and it may be hard to change that at first, but it is not impossible. You are more than capable of rewiring your brain. It's *your* brain after all. *Your* brain, *your* life, *your* choices and no one else's. If you have not been able to change your habits and mindset yet but have tried and tried in the past, it's not because you're incapable of doing it, it's because you haven't found the right method yet and that's ok. Everyone is different. Every journey is different. What worked for me and for others may not work for everyone and people will struggle until they know better and change when they can do better. I absolutely believe that.

So, there you have it. Now that you have taken a better look at your mindset and what your current thoughts are telling you and why, you should have a better understanding of how your brain works to either hinder you or help you. Spend some time reflecting on your mindset and get yourself pumped for change by finding some mindset reset videos, self-help podcasts, blogs, articles or books and deep dive for inspiration and information (wink-wink, nudge-nudge you can find links to all of that in the back of this book). In the next section, we will dive deeper into your mindset by uncovering your limiting beliefs that are holding you back, looking at what you instead want to think and feel. Then we will explore some ways to flip your switch and rewire your thinking to believe in yourself and your innate capability to change and function to the best of your ability.

"Probably the biggest insight… is that happiness is not just a place, but also a process. Happiness is an ongoing process of fresh challenges, and it takes the right attitudes and activities to continue to be happy."

~ Ed Diener

"Happiness is not out there for us to find. The reason that it's not out there is that it's inside us."

~ Sonja Lyubomirsky

"The primary cause of unhappiness is never the situation, but your thoughts about it. Be aware of the thoughts you are thinking."

~ Eckhart Tolle

PART TWO

I Object: Breaking the mental barriers of limiting beliefs

We are now ready to dive deeper into identifying your limiting beliefs by writing down specific views that are hindering your growth, happiness, and success and flip them to uncover how you want to think and feel instead. To identify your limiting beliefs, you must start by becoming aware of the recurring thoughts or self-talk that undermine your confidence and prevent you from taking action. To overcome that which is holding you back, you must challenge these ideas by questioning their validity and exploring alternative perspectives that lift you, rather than pull you down. It's time to stop berating yourself and begin sticking up for yourself against yourself. So, let's get started.

Step 1: If you have the PDF download then you've got the format right there ready to go. If not and you're working on your own book, prepare your page by ruling a line down the middle to create two columns. Label the left side "Limiting Beliefs" and the right side "What I want to think/feel." On the limiting beliefs side, write all the things you say and think about yourself negatively or want to change. This might be things like: I'm overweight but diets don't work for me, I'm lazy but that's just how I am, I'm time-poor but am always too busy and can't change that, I'm disorganised no matter how hard I try to keep on top of things, I'm reactive and that's just how I am because I'm just like my parent, I'm depressed/anxious but can't change because I'm wired that way, I'm always stressed/overwhelmed because life is so hectic and always will be, people don't like me or I'm not a good person, I'm too stuck to change or it's too late for me, I'm too young/old/sick/traumatised, I'm financially struggling but will always be poor, I'm stuck in a job I hate but have no option but to keep it for the money, I'm a bad parent/partner/friend/employee etc.

Don't get too carried away and go digging for every little flaw and insecurity and make this a self-slamming exercise. This is WWE of the mind. Just focus on the main things that are core beliefs and attitudes towards yourself as they arise often or are things you identify yourself with. Please know, that this is not about eliciting shame and blame, it is about recognising how this makes you feel and what items on this list are a reflection of actual aspects of your life (that you can change) or just lies you tell yourself (that we can shift your mindset on). In the PDF there are two pages provided but you don't need to fill it all out. There is an additional page so as you start to get better at recognising your limiting beliefs, you can come back to this and write more down if you'd like to keep a record of what you are working to change.

On the other side of the sheet, you are going to line up your negative thoughts or limiting beliefs with who you are when you get past the lie you're telling yourself or who you inspire to become by making changes in your life to redirect those negative things to a more positive outlook. To use the example above, this might look something like:

- I'm overweight (becomes) I want to be a healthy weight and love my body.
- I'm lazy (becomes) I want to feel productive and accomplished.
- I'm time-poor (becomes) I want more time for enjoyment/more control over my time.
- I'm disorganised (becomes) I want to be more organised.
- I'm reactive (becomes) I want to be more emotionally stable and mature.
- I'm depressed (becomes) I want to feel happy.

- I'm anxious (becomes) I want to be confident and relaxed in life and out in the world.
- I'm always stressed/overwhelmed (becomes) I want calm and relaxation.
- People don't like me (becomes) I want to stop feeling like my worth is tethered to the approval of others.
- I'm too stuck to change or it's too late for me (becomes) I have the power to change at any point.
- I'm too young/old/sick (becomes) it's never too late or early to work towards what I want.
- I'm financially struggling (becomes) money is everywhere and available for me to make in many ways.
- I've been through so much it's changed me (becomes) I don't want to be shaped by my past.
- I'm stuck in a job I hate (becomes) I can pick the job I do and can find one I enjoy and feel purpose in
- I'm a bad parent/partner/friend/employee etc. (becomes) I want to be the best person I can for the people who I love and value.

Step two: Let's have a quick look at some of these things. Put an * (asterisk) next to the things you can physically work on to change and a heart by the things you understand are only how you see yourself and require a mindset shift around (hint: everything on your list should have a heart next to them because even the things you can change physically require mindset shifts to do the work and take action). Things like body weight, your job, emotional issues, organisation, and time management all require both a mindset shift and physical action.

For example:

- With losing or gaining weight don't think about it changing the way you look to be more attractive or accepted by others, redirect your intention to becoming healthier to prolong your life and to *feeling* more energised and confident to do things that you may be restricted from because of weight.
- With your job, stop focusing on what you don't like and start thinking about your real desires. Tell yourself: I am not stuck in this job, but I will do it for now for an income WHILE I work towards finding a job I like. Then take action and start your job search journey right now! Need new qualifications to do the job you dream of or want to work for yourself? Start looking into how to do it and even if it might take years to get that qualification shift your

mindset from "why bother when it will take so long before I can even be qualified" to "even if I study for ten years it will be worth it to be in my dream job from then on for the rest of my life and that is 100% better than working my whole life in a job I hate."

- With your emotions, mental health, and trauma you might need a lot of support and work to heal, and what you need may be highly individual to your needs and your situation. However, no matter what you've been through one thing is the same for everyone who has suffered through traumatic situations; the healing journey is a long road, but you can do it and it starts now. It starts here with you taking action to shift your mindset to serve you. Through working through this book, reading other self-help and healing content, therapy, and mental health support programs, you can heal and change if you put your mind in the right place to do it.

For things like: People don't like me, I'm too young/old/sick, I'm too stuck to change, it's too late for me or I'm a bad parent/partner/friend/employee etc., these are things that need a mindset shift to get past these beliefs. Being a "bad" parent/partner etc., is a thought based on your own reflection of yourself. You may need to do things to change the physical aspects of your life making you feel that way BUT the idea that you are defined as a person by your mistakes and flaws is a fallacy you need to get past. People don't like me is usually a lie you tell yourself because of how *you* view yourself and how you view yourself is based on a mixture of the mistreatment of others in the past and your own cognitive distortions. You think you're weird, awkward, different, or whatever it is that makes you think you know what others think and feel. Most people don't hate you. Most people aren't thinking of you at all because they have their own lives and problems and if they are using their time and energy to focus on you and your life then that's a shame for them. That's their problem with their own flaws and negative perceptions of what life is. Healed people don't focus on the negative in themselves or others. Good people don't bring others down for any reason so if there are people in your life doing that, let them go and let their opinions stay over there with them. Oh, and as for being too old/young/stuck to change. Rubbish! Your brain is the supercomputer of the human condition and can rewire itself and form new synaptic connections to create new habits, solidify new knowledge and completely change right from the moment you're born to the day you die. This is not my opinion or magical, wishful thinking; this is cold, hard facts based on science.

Step 3: Now that you have taken some time to identify your limiting beliefs, here are eight steps to take to challenge them, flip them on their head, grind them into dust under your feet and then reshape them into the beautiful confident perspectives you need to move forward and shift your mindset for happiness and success. In your PDF or notebook, pick two or three of the limiting beliefs you identified that you think are the biggest obstacles holding you back and use them to them for the following steps.

Question the Evidence: Let's first examine the evidence supporting your limiting beliefs. Are there concrete facts or experiences that validate these beliefs, or are they based on assumptions or past failures? Do you know what automatic negative thoughts are? Dr Daniel Amen, a renowned American psychiatrist and brain disorder specialist calls these ANTs, and you can squish them by asking: "Is this true? Do I have real evidence to support this thought, belief, or claim?" If the answer is no, then squish it and flip it to "how would I feel if I didn't have this thought" and "what if the opposite was true?" Challenge the validity of the evidence and consider alternative perspectives and while this might seem at first like you are lying to yourself because your brain is so cemented in its negative reality, in time you will change your own mind.

Consider the Consequences: Reflect on how your limiting beliefs impact your behaviour, emotions, and overall well-being. Would you be happier if you weren't constantly bringing yourself down? Would you be more involved with your kids if you weren't stuck thinking you'll never change or that you don't have the time? Would you have taken a chance that could have led to happiness and financial success if you didn't have that belief holding you back? Would you feel more confident and go out more or express yourself better if not for those negative thoughts about yourself and what people think of you? Recognise how these beliefs hold you back from pursuing your goals or living a fulfilling life.

Seek Counterexamples: Look for evidence that contradicts your limiting beliefs. Identify instances where you have succeeded, overcome challenges, or demonstrated the opposite of what your belief suggests. You are not a failure. You are not useless. There are amazing things you do every day and things you constantly accomplish and get right but you're overlooking them in favour of focusing on the negative. For example, you might often feel like you're not getting enough done because you have this never-ending to-do list and there is a huge part of it not getting ticked off. Reality check: a to-do list never ends and there will always be a Brontosaurus's-butt-sized load of stuff you need to or want to accomplish. Don't focus on what you haven't done, look at what you have achieved including all the mundane everyday tasks you have to do outside of the extra things on your to-do lists. Most people forget that stuff takes time too. A fun and effective way to seek counterexamples is to get a little split-personality crazy and when you start running yourself down with one of your limiting beliefs, your inner lawyer should jump to your own defence and start finding examples to prove that what you're saying is not true. Use these counterexamples of success and achievement to challenge the validity of your limiting beliefs.

Reframe Negative Thoughts: Practice reframing negative thoughts into more empowering and realistic statements. A simple way to do this is to flip it to the complete opposite. Instead of saying "I'm not good enough," reframe it as "I am capable and deserving of success." Instead of thinking "I can't change" say "I have the natural ability to learn new things at any point in my life -

science says so." As mentioned earlier, negative thought patterns and habitual ways of thinking are already solidified in your mind to be automatic responses to known situations. Your brain has done the work to solidify these things into an automatic response so now you must do the work to set the new responses. Keep at it regularly and persistently, replacing self-critical language with affirmations that promote self-confidence and resilience. Remember this takes time and practice to make it a new habit.

Test Your Beliefs: Challenge your limiting beliefs by testing them through small, manageable actions. Take incremental steps outside of your comfort zone to see if your beliefs hold true or if they are as exaggerated as the stories of that one relative at family gatherings. Additionally, don't take on too much at once and get overwhelmed. Instead of addressing every limiting belief and every bad habit and trying to turn it all around at once, focus on one or two things at a time and work on taking little steps towards your eventual desired outcome – no one eats an entire pizza in one bite so don't bite off more than you can chew, choke and blame the pizza. Small changes and tiny steps may take a long time but not doing anything or giving up keeps you stuck in the same spot which is worse. So, take the tiny steps, get the little wins, celebrate all progress no matter how small the increments and use these experiences as evidence to reshape your beliefs.

Seek Alternative Explanations: As our limiting beliefs come from past experiences or the opinions and actions of others, you need to consider alternative explanations for negative experiences, past failures or setbacks that don't reinforce your limiting beliefs. For example, instead of looking at a failure as a reflection of your intelligence or capability and feeling guilt and shame about it, recognise that at the time you were doing the best you could with the knowledge you had. Also, look at why you may have failed at something and instead focus on what you did wrong, explore what valuable lessons and experience was gained. Regarding the opinions and actions of others, instead of telling yourself they feel or act a certain way because you are no good or failing them, understand that other people's problems are a reflection of their inner self. Even if you did do something to hurt someone in the past, you can't change that it happened, but you can learn to do better and not exhibit the same behaviours again. Take time to explore external factors, situations, or temporary setbacks that may have contributed to outcomes instead of attributing it solely to personal inadequacy.

Challenge Perfectionism: Recognise that perfectionism often fuels limiting beliefs by setting unrealistic standards – like expecting your cat to listen to your instructions at all times. Perfectionism isn't a form of excellence to strive for but is instead a fear of failure wrapped in insecurity with a heaping side of anxiety. You do not need to be perfect. You do not need to always succeed and avoid failure, struggles and setbacks at all times. You must take the idea that failures and imperfect action means you *are* a failure or not good enough and instead acknowledge that anyone taking action and trying is 100% ahead of anyone not getting anywhere because they think they must be perfect to even start. Embrace imperfection and view failure as a natural part of the learning process. Shift your focus from avoiding failure to embracing the growth and progress it brings to your life.

Cultivate Self-Compassion: This is the most important step of all because being unkind to yourself throughout any process of change is only going to hinder you, hold you back and make things more uncomfortable than they need to be. Practice self-compassion by treating yourself with kindness and understanding. Acknowledge that everyone struggles with self-doubt and imperfections. Even the most successful people in the world have flaws and have experienced failure repeatedly. What denotes success is not the absence of failure but persistence, resilience, and belief in your abilities despite the challenges and setbacks. Ask anyone who made it to their ultimate dream life, and they will tell you about that time they spilled coffee all over their fancy white suit and had to deliver a TED talk in their underwear just like the reoccurring nightmare predicted they would. Offer yourself the same empathy and support you would offer to a friend facing similar challenges because you deserve the same amount of love and respect from yourself.

Step 4: If you want to go more in-depth here, the PDF provides a few extra blank lined pages (as does your notebook) to reflect on each of the previous steps in more detail and allows you to plan for how you might challenge those beliefs and reframe your way of thinking. For number one if you write down a belief such as "I'm overweight and diets never work" and you've said yes that's true because the evidence is the number on the scales and the failure of all the diets you've tried in the past, you need to now write down how to change this. Make a mini plan that shows you understand that maybe your diet lacked consistency. Maybe you need to stick to it for 12 months or more to see impactful change. Perhaps it was too much too fast so you should focus first on changing breakfast to healthy food for a few weeks then lunch then dinner then snacks. Maybe you were losing a little weight in slow increments, but your mindset and impatience told you it was too little too slow, so you convinced yourself it wasn't working. Think very carefully about these things and use the advice from number eight when you do this by imagining, how would I talk to or advise a friend about this.

Now that you have completed this exercise, don't just leave it, and forget. Spend some time reflecting on what you've learned and written down. Maybe go deeper by looking for inspirational videos, empowering music, and other things to help lift you and keep you motivated to change. If you're looking to implement a diet or workout routine find information to help. If you want to quit smoking or drinking outline a plan and look for support and information to assist you with that. If you're thinking of training that crocodile I'm sure you'll find something online and if not then go ahead and wing it then write about it to inspire others when you're done. Whatever it is you've identified here and want to work on, make sure you come back to this list and reflect on what you feel and what you want to change. Focus on that deep, innate feeling within you that knows you need to make the changes and instead of concentrating on the pain of guilt and shame, realise that you will continue to feel that way if you don't take action. Then, redirect your focus to imagining how it will feel to achieve your goals and be the person you want to be.

It is essential to *feel* the emotions associated with success as part of the process of rewiring your brain and nervous system to help you succeed. Feel what it would be like to be healthy, happy, in a job you love, in a healthy relationship or to be confident, calm, and content. Research in behavioural psychology shows that having thoughts alone doesn't change things, having feelings alone doesn't shift things, but combine your positive thoughts with positive emotions and watch your world transform almost like magic (but it's not magic; it's real-life science remember). In a research study conducted by cellular biologist Glen Phein PhD at the HeartMath Research Centre in California, scientists examined three groups of people to see if they could literally unwind strands of DNA with thoughts and feelings. Thoughts or feelings alone didn't help but those who combined intentions with positive feelings changed the DNA. Other studies show that with positive emotions and intentions you can change your gene expression and heal from past trauma. People across the world in scientific studies have improved their brain and physical health (proven from brain scans and other medical tests) through the power of rewiring your thoughts. This is called the placebo effect, and it is powerful and real with a multitude of studies and research to prove it.

The power of your mind is so amazing. Clinical studies have proven that negative thoughts trigger the release of stress chemicals and hormones that damage your body, while positive thoughts trigger the release of beneficial neurotransmitters such as serotonin and dopamine. So, it's not just philosophical but physiological evidence that shows your powerful mind can either bring you down or empower you; it can make you feel well or manifest physical symptoms of illness and disease in your body and which of those things it does is up to you. The only person or thing that has full control of what it does, at the core of all things, is you. Remember that you are the architect of your own destiny. You are the captain of your ship navigating the ocean of your life – just look out for icebergs because those things are sneaky. Most importantly, remember that assessing your current mindset is an ongoing practice that requires patience and self-compassion. Be gentle with yourself as you explore your thoughts and feelings and above all, believe in yourself and your ability to make true change, because I believe in you and know you can do it. Let's get ready for the next steps.

"Whole life is a search for beauty. But, when the beauty is found inside, the search ends and a beautiful journey begins."

~ Harshit Walia

"It is a predisposition of human nature to consider an unpleasant idea untrue, and then it is easy to find arguments against it."

~ Sigmund Freud

"As for the future, it remains unwritten. Anything can happen and often we are wrong. The best we can do with the future is prepare and savour the possibilities of what can be done in the present."

~ Todd Kashdan

PART THREE

Paint Your Future with Purpose: Who do you want to be?

Now that you've done the work to assess your mindset and delved into identifying and challenging your limiting beliefs, you will have a deeper understanding of who you are and who you want to be. It's time to define a clear vision for the mindset you want to cultivate. To do this, you must visualise how you would think, feel, and act with a more positive, resilient, and growth-oriented outlook for life. Identifying a clear vision for the mindset you want to cultivate is a powerful step toward personal growth and development because once you clearly define how you want to think and feel, you can do the conscious work to shift your thinking to align with who you want to be. How do you do that? Well, this is an instructional book, after all, and we're not just here to learn—we're here to take action! So, grab your PDF printout or personal book, flex those writing muscles, and let's get started with defining who you want to be as a person. Think of it like creating your own superhero identity – minus the spandex (unless that's your thing, no judgment here).

Step 1: To start, you need to reflect on your core values in what defines you as a person underneath the surface of all your struggles and flaws (real or perceived). You may identify the term core values with places like schools and other organisations that often boast things like respect, honesty, resilience etc as their core values. But it's not just organisations like these that should identify and reflect core values. Every person should also do the same for themselves to define who they are or who they want to be.

Most people do this without even thinking of it in this sense by professing things like "I'm an honest/loyal/kind/empathetic person." Consider what values are most important to you. These could be those qualities just mentioned or others like resilience, critical thinking, creativity, enthusiasm, entertainment, fun or anything else that defines your character or beliefs about what makes you, you. Your mindset should align with these values, so if you consider yourself a hard worker and resilient, you will not give up easily or let struggles get in your way. Once you've thought about what your core values are or would be if you were to become the person you strive to be, write them down on the Define Your Vision page in the PDF printout or on the next page of your book under a heading such as: "My Core Values."

Step 2: Once you've done that, it's time to identify the desired traits that align with your core values. Think about the specific traits or characteristics you want to embody. For example, if one of your core values is resilience then you might strive to be more optimistic, proactive, flexible, or self-confident. If a core value is kindness you might strive to be open-minded, a good listener, accepting, and patient. Write each core value with a list of desired traits beside them that align with that value and as you do, think about how it would feel to actively engage in these behaviours and have a mindset that aligns with these traits.

It is essential to take the time to visualise your ideal self and mentally step into the role of who you ultimately want to be. This is called mental rehearsal and is a proven self-improvement strategy based in behavioural psychology. Envision yourself embodying the mindset you desire and think about how you would feel and act if you were the kind, patient, resilient, emotionally competent, confident [insert any desired trait] person you aspire to be. Picture yourself being so resilient that you could bounce back from a bad hair day without flinching, or so kind that even your grumpy neighbour starts to smile when they see you. You're basically crafting a blueprint for a super-you – no cape required (unless, of course, you're really into capes as well).

Imagine how you would think, feel, and act in various situations that might challenge you or present you with opportunities. What would super-you do? For example, would a brave, confident person shy away from a challenge or opportunity that could transform their life just because it also had a risk of failure, a difficult choice, or a change to make? No way! That's why you're here taking these steps to transform your life despite challenges and a lot of hard work because you are brave and confident. Remember, confidence is not competence; it is simply the willingness to try.

Now see yourself embodying and enacting all the behaviours and beliefs you truly want to align with. This will feel foreign at first after thinking and feeling a certain way for so long but mentally rehearsing yourself achieving your goals and feeling the potential and purpose of your desires is an essential part of transforming your mindset. The more you do it, the more natural it feels to be aligned with the new version of you. Plus, research shows the significance of using mental rehearsal and intentions together to make physical transformations in your mind and body. When you think about something, it signals your body to feel a certain way. If you think about things that make you sad or frustrated, it signals your nervous system to release the relevant hormones and chemicals to induce a feeling in your body. The same is true for when you think about good things, happy things, and positive transformations in your life. The trick here is to practice, practice, practice. Because your brain and body have been conditioned to the negative for so long, you must work for a while to switch it to the positive. With time and patience, it will shift.

Step 3: It's time to set some clear goals that define specific, measurable objectives related to your mindset. These could include daily habits, such as practising gratitude or mindfulness if your core values aim to be something like patience, calmness, resilience, or emotional regulation. You can even set larger objectives, such as completing a challenging project with a positive attitude if your desired traits are persistence, hard-working, enthusiasm or something related. If you strive to be a fit healthy person, you might take action to incorporate a 5-minute workout every morning until you can make it 15 or 30 minutes, a walk around the block each afternoon or focus on breakfast being your healthy meal of the day before working your way up to lunch and dinner. Write down a few small goals and actions you can take to make tangible changes in your life and mindset to align with each core value and think about how you can start incorporating these into your everyday life.

Be careful here though because you don't want to be overwhelmed – remember what we said about biting off more pizza than you can chew. Although the PDF print out provides plenty of space for you to work with, every little thing you list here does not need goals, plans, and action right now and all at once. With anything, small steps and bite-sized pieces are the key to change. While you might identify several areas for change and write out plans and actions for all your core values, you will only need to commit to one or two things to start working on now and work your way through your goals over time.

Look closely at what you want to work on and identify one or two most important areas to focus on that will significantly help shift your mindset for the better. Traits such as emotional regulation, confidence, time management skills and organisation are things that can make life and other goals a lot easier. Start with these core things and focus on them then eventually, you will see things shifting more swiftly as you get good at altering your mindset over time. You will start to find that one thing will impact the next and before you know it, you'll be a completely different person with a new outlook and a new personality, and you'll be a force to be reckoned with.

Step 4: Now it's time to create some positive affirmations that align with who you want to be. You can use some of the examples on the affirmations page at the beginning of the PDF and the end of this book or jump online and look some up to use if you don't want to create your own. Search "affirmations for [resilience, honesty, patience etc]" and pick ones that resonate with you. These don't have to be airy-fairy fluff and stuff; they can be long or short, fun, and quirky or meaningful and serious. You decide.

They can even be a little cheer you sing in your head. ("Helsy, Helsy you're the bomb, you can vibe good all day long!") When I was first going through these big changes (and I still do this now), I'd sing little lines from songs to myself all the time but change the lyrics to align with what I was doing. Not to brag but, I am the absolute champ of spur-of-the-moment, on-the-spot parody singing. Bring the fun to get it done is one of the mottos I coined, and it is the best advice I can give you in almost any challenging moment. No matter how you do it or what form this takes, it is an extremely beneficial tool to develop positive affirmations that reinforce your desired mindset.

There is only one hard fast rule here: no putting yourself down or slandering yourself. It's okay to swear at yourself if you're like, "Come on bitch you can do this because you know you are one amazing muthafucker," but you are not to call yourself a lazy bitch, a dumb shit, or tell yourself to get your fat useless arse into gear. This is not tough love. This is not helpful. This is the negative mindset, and it has no place here in this magical, profound transformation you are undertaking. Rule of thumb, if you wouldn't say it to a loved one to motivate them, don't say it to yourself to guilt or shame yourself into doing the work. Now, once you've decided on some things you can tell yourself in the moments when you commonly struggle, write them down and repeat them regularly to reinforce your vision and shift your thinking patterns. You can also put them on little posters on the walls of your home if that helps you.

Step 5: Now that you're developing a good understanding of the values you want to embody, the traits you need to develop and ways you can take action and reinforce your mindset to achieve these outcomes, a great way to stay on track is to seek inspiration from others. While social media can be bad for you in a lot of ways and it gets a bad rap for a lot of very valid reasons, it can also be an amazing tool when utilised correctly. Get on your social accounts and follow people who talk about and share knowledge that inspires you to be your best, such as mindset coaches, motivational speakers and others who embody the characteristics and values you wish to achieve. Look for role models or mentors who exemplify the mindset you aspire to cultivate, find them on YouTube and TikTok and listen to their videos and podcasts.

Instead of letting other people's success make you feel like you are less, be inspired by their words and accomplishments. Look at what they are doing, thinking, and feeling and tell yourself you can do that and be that too. Learn from their experiences and practices to gain insights and motivation because most of the people you admire succeeded through countless struggles and setbacks and so many successful people worked their way up from nothing. Take a moment right now to do a little searching and make a list in your book or PDF of the people, pages, books, podcasts etc you can follow for information and inspiration and where to go to find them – don't forget the list of links in the back of this book for your friendly neighbourhood Helsy.

Now that you have assessed your core values, decided who you want to be and taken some actionable steps towards aligning your goals with the mindset you want to cultivate, it is crucial to be kind to yourself throughout this process. Embracing a new mindset will involve setbacks and challenges and it will involve falling back into old habits and old ways of thinking over and over until you solidify the new patterns and thoughts. Even once you get good at thinking better, the old you will creep back from time to time but less frequently and with less power and authority over your mind and feelings.

That is because your brain automatically reverts to what is familiar. You must not let this discourage you or convince yourself you're failing or not able to commit but instead acknowledge that this is part of the process. You *can* commit. You *are* capable and change takes time. Your brain is working against you for now, so you must take conscious control of it and retrain it to instead work *for* you. In time, with repetition and most importantly with care and compassion, your automatic thoughts and feelings will flip to serve you and all your hard work and patience will be so worth it. In the meantime, treating yourself with compassion and understanding will help you stay resilient and committed to your long-term goal of wholeness, peace, and contentment.

It is also important that throughout this process of change and mindset reset you allow yourself to evaluate your progress and adjust when needed. Your plans don't always go as you want them to and that's okay. Plans and goals are not fixed but are guidelines that help light the way on a path that flows and ebbs like water. Just go with the flow and surf the waves life rolls in – if you face plant in the water you can always get back up and keep going. Have a goal in mind and a plan to follow but if you need to change something or meet a challenge or set back, roll with it, and know that things are still working for you as long as you stay resilient, believe in your ability to get to where you're going and be gentle with yourself along the way. Regularly assess your progress and adjust your approach as needed. Stay flexible and open to new insights and be willing to modify your vision as you learn and grow.

Finally, and most importantly you must always continue to celebrate your successes. This aligns with our earlier approach to challenging limiting beliefs in which we shift our focus from failures and challenges and home in on success to counter beliefs of failure and incompetence. You must always acknowledge and celebrate the milestones you achieve along the way, and I don't just mean big shiny achievements but every, single, little, win. You're trying to be a morning person and you got up after 3 snooze hits instead of 5... do a happy dance all the way to the bathroom baby and know that tomorrow you're getting up after 2 because you're a rockstar. You're trying to be less reactive, and you only ruminated on that jerk who cut you off in traffic for the next two blocks instead of all the way to work… hip-hip-hurray honey you're smashing it today. Recognizing your progress reinforces positive behaviours and encourages continued growth. Understanding that progress isn't just big and obvious but can be small as well helps shift your focus to see that you are often achieving way more than you realise.

So, you now understand that to embody and enact the traits aligned with your core values, it is essential to mentally rehearse yourself taking action to be that person. You must recognise who you are and who you want to be and create small manageable goals to work towards achieving success in these areas you've identified. Be patient and compassionate with yourself and seek inspiration from others who embody the values you want to live by, instead of feeling inadequate by their standards. Go with the flow when challenges present themselves and above all be sure to celebrate every tiny win with enthusiasm and joy. By following these steps, you can define a clear vision for the mindset you want to cultivate and take meaningful steps towards creating that vision in your daily life. You are now ready to go forth to take the next steps to a more positive mindset by becoming even more aware of who you are and who you want to be in the next section of the book.

"Becoming is better than being."

~ Carol S. Dweck

"To find out what is truly individual in ourselves, profound reflection is needed; and suddenly we realise how uncommonly difficult the discovery of individuality is."

~ C.G. Jung

"Once you start making the effort to wake yourself up – that is, be more mindful in your activities – you suddenly start appreciating life a lot more."

~ Robert Biswas-Diener

PART FOUR

Mirror, Mirror on the wall: Who am I behind it all?

At the beginning of this book, we took a deep dive into the core of you by assessing your current mindset because that is the first major step in becoming aware of who you are and who you want to be. But being self-aware isn't just about stopping to become familiar with your thoughts and feelings once but learning how to do it consciously and frequently. Notice I do not say, "at all times?" That is because we have a brain that wants to automate so much for ease and to save energy, so it is impossible to be aware and conscious all the time. Some of the time you will still slip into auto-piolet and relapse into old ways of thinking but the more you practice cultivating a sense of self-awareness, the easier it becomes to recognise when you are out of sync or falling into the trap of negative thinking and old patterns.

You must develop self-awareness by observing your thoughts, emotions, and reactions throughout the day. Notice any patterns of negative self-talk, self-doubt, or limiting beliefs that arise and what situations, places or people trigger these negative thoughts and emotions. By completing the exercises in the previous sections to become aware of limiting beliefs, deciding how you want to flip them to serve you, and identifying your core values and what traits and behaviours you need to change and exhibit to embody them, you're already on your way to becoming more self-aware.

You now have tools in your mental toolbox to help you practice keeping a check on your negative thoughts and feelings and to combat them and transform them into a more positive outlook. For example, when you start to feel yourself getting a little stressed and overwhelmed, stop, and take a moment to think about where you are and what you're doing. Think about the thoughts going through your head and work out if you are subconsciously saying or doing things that are contrary to what you want to think, feel and be. Then use your mental tool kit to flip the thoughts, reprogram the script, use one of your chosen affirmations or give yourself a little pep talk to get you back on track.

Another way to become more self-aware is through using mindfulness techniques to become more present and aware of your inner dialogue. While some forms of mindfulness (or more particularly some ways these techniques are framed and talked about) might turn people off and even make them laugh and think it's silly, mindfulness is about being present in the moment, calming your system and, yes you guessed it, being more self-aware. Mindfulness can be as simple as pausing and taking the time to bring yourself into your present moment, recognising if you are stressing about time, the past, the future, old limiting beliefs, or negative thoughts. However, there are many other techniques such as journalling, intentional breathing, setting intentions and practising gratitude that can help you become more self-aware. They're not hard to do either. Let's explore a few things you can do. You can complete the worksheet on the Practicing Self-Awareness page of the PDF or in your book write down your ideas and reflections on these mindfulness techniques that you will start to utilise to practice self-awareness every day.

1. Mindfulness Meditation:

Regular meditation practice can not only help you observe your thoughts and emotions without judgment, but it is also a beneficial tool for regulating your nervous system, decreasing stress and anxiety, and recharging your batteries. In an upcoming guide, we will deep dive into meditation, how to do it and the benefits you receive but there are a lot of short, guided meditations you can start accessing online right now. You don't need complete peace and quiet and you don't need an hour or even half an hour. Some are five or ten minutes long and help to calm and reset your mind when you need it most.

If you have a mind that is always racing, don't think meditation is not for you as your mind never stops. I used to laugh at the idea of meditating and the very concept of "clearing your mind of all thoughts" (as if that could ever be possible for a whirling, swirling, chaotic brain like mine). Having thoughts during meditation is perfectly ok and sometimes the point (you don't need to clear your mind and sit cross-legged saying ummmmmmmmm over and over). If you've never meditated before, you'd be surprised how easy and nice it is.

There are many ways to meditate such as in a sitting position, laying down, standing or even while walking and awake. You might have silence or music or listen to a guided meditation where someone talks you through focusing on your breath and awareness. You might do visualisation meditation where you focus on a specific area of your life you want to change spend some time visualising what that looks like for you when you do. Meditation is not one thing or one size fits all so it might just be about trying different techniques and finding the right way for you. Just don't fall into the trap of doing it once or only a few times and fobbing it off as a lost cause. Do it for at least 5-10 minutes once a day for two weeks and see how you feel. Even if you're not a meditating Zen master by then, I bet you'll have gained some experience and benefits from it and are changing your mind about the very concept of meditation.

Meditation is not just a way to relax and clear your mind but a great opportunity for mentally rehearsing your ideal future, goal outcomes and mindset shift to help solidify new ways of thinking and new possibilities in your life. So, take five minutes to listen to a guided meditation, relax your body, breathe, and start developing a non-reactive awareness of your inner experiences, to better understand the patterns and tendencies of your mind.

Take action in your workbook: Look up some meditation methods you think will work with you and your lifestyle. Hint: don't focus on what works with your current lifestyle too much but try to work with the vision of who you want to be. If you want to be more present, calm and mindful and less stressed, overwhelmed and time poor don't think you don't have time or the capability to do this. Think to yourself, a calm, mindful person would be able to do this and would establish dedicated time each day to meditate. List your ideas and information here under the title 'Mindfulness Meditation.'

2. Journaling:

It is a great idea to keep a journal to reflect on your thoughts, feelings, and experiences. Even if it is just a quick jotting at the end of the day, writing can help you gain clarity and insight into your mindset, allowing you to identify limiting beliefs or negative thought patterns that may be holding you back. A really easy way to use journalling to help you be more aware of your thoughts and feelings is to divide your page in two, write all the things that went well down one side and all the times you felt things going wrong or slipped into old ways down the other. BUT, as you write the negative things down, try to understand the reason why you felt that way and how you could feel better, flip the script, or improve next time.

Here's an example from my own life as I often find myself slipping into old beliefs that I am not doing enough or keeping on top of what I want to do (or *feel* like I *should* be doing). "I was feeling overwhelmed with all the household tasks *BUT* I will recognise that I had other things to prioritise and focus on as well so will not let guilt take over me. I can recognise what tasks to prioritise, that I can't always do everything all at once and that this helps me stay in control of my time and energy."

Take action in your workbook: If journaling is something you want to start doing (and one I highly recommend for beneficial reflection) write down your ideas about it in your workbook. Some people do not like to write and that is ok. You can type your daily journal entries on a computer, do a private video diary or commit to sharing your experiences and growth with others on social media by doing daily journal videos. You can also use your phone's voice recording app and chat about your day, experiences and what you are learning and progressing with. However, you do it, research shows that journaling, reflecting and recording your thoughts, feelings and progress helps significantly shift your attitudes and behaviors to align with your goals and aspirations.

3. Self-Reflection:

Set aside time regularly to reflect on your goals, values, and priorities and home in on all the successes and progress you are constantly making. Consider whether your thoughts and actions align with what is truly important to you and adjust as needed to stay on course. While this can also tie in with journalling, if you're not the journalling type this can be a good one to do internally. Instead of checking your emails or social media in the morning when you have breakfast, instead, use this time to reflect on your progress and plan for improvement where necessary. If you are not setting aside regular time for reflection, at least do it when you are starting to feel overwhelmed or have old patterns and negative thoughts creeping in.

When I start to feel that familiar stress, lack, impatience, or time blindness creeping up like a ninja in the night, I take a moment to write down all the ways I know I'm succeeding and progressing. I jot down my newly rewired thoughts around previous limiting beliefs. This exercise reaffirms my new outlook on issues like being time-poor, feeling lacking, or thinking I'm not doing enough to reach my goals and full potential. And guess what? It significantly shifts my mindset! I start to feel so much better, reigniting that spark for potential and growth. It's like giving my brain a pep talk: "Hey, you! Remember all those awesome things you're doing? Yeah, you're crushing it!" Before I know it,

I'm back on track, ready to take on the world – or at least daily to-do list.

Take action in your workbook: Write down what time of day you will set aside or plan for reflection then note a few key areas you want to focus on for progress and to be aware of how you are doing and what else needs work.

4. Set Intentions:

Start each day by setting positive intentions for how you want to think, feel, and behave. If you've noticed lately you are slipping into negative thoughts about the past or future, make an intention that today I will focus only on what today will bring and what is happening right now. If you've been getting impatient with your kids or partner, make the intention for the day to pause and breathe if you feel irritated, count to three and then choose your words and reactions more carefully. If you forget and lash out then walk away, take a moment to think about how you could have handled it differently and come back with a clear head, an apology, and an explanation for how you feel and why you want to try to do better.

I do this with my kids when I am overwhelmed and react poorly – I'm at the point now when that is very infrequent and when it does happen it's usually at bedtime on a school night when they're fluffing around. I come back and say something like, "I'm sorry I yelled and reacted that way. I don't want to feel like that, but I was getting overwhelmed when you were not going to bed on time. I am working on better controlling my feelings and reactions and that is my part, but your part is making sure you are getting to bed by the appropriate time for us both to get the sleep and rest we need. When you don't go to bed on time, I don't get to bed on time which means you are making a choice that not only impacts your sleep but mine too."

Don't feel guilty or like you've failed if you don't always live up to your intentions. The goal here is to try and the more you try the better you get. You're not going to always remember your intentions in the beginning, but practice makes you better (notice I didn't say perfect because perfection is a lie and a toxic expectation). Another thing to remember is you are not a machine. Don't try to set multiple intentions to work on at once because remembering to change one thing is hard enough without adding unnecessary work to the mental pile. Pick the most important thing for you now and make your intentions focused on things you need to be aware of for the most impactful change. For me, it's often being aware of my emotional reactions because this is something I struggled with my entire life and is a foundational tool for many other things to be intentional about. By consciously directing your focus and energy towards positive outcomes, you can cultivate a more optimistic and resilient mindset.

Take action in your workbook: Identify the key areas you are focusing on for the most impactful change to your everyday life and well-being (i.e. emotional responses, kindness, organization, quitting a bad habit etc.) and note down some intentions you will set to remind yourself of who you are and what you're working towards. Example: Today I choose to slow down and be aware of how I feel so I have better control over my emotional responses.

5. Practice Gratitude:

Cultivating an attitude of gratitude by regularly acknowledging and appreciating the good things in your life is the key ingredient to a healthy mindset and an abundant life. Being aware of all the small things life presents us with that are good, beautiful, amazing, and helpful to us can help you be more aware of the better things in life when the negative thoughts and feelings are creeping in. This can be as simple as choosing to focus on the good things in life, the moments that we appreciate with our kids, friends, and family, or even the pleasant shopkeeper who brightens your day when you're in their store.

We have more to be grateful for than we realise because so often we let the bad outweigh the good and sometimes miss the little things to appreciate because society has cultivated a mindset focused on only being grateful when we are succeeding, making lots of money, fit and healthy or in happy relationships. Even in times of struggle and lack there are so many things to be grateful for and recognising them is one of the key ingredients for getting yourself out of those negative situations and patterns of thought. Becoming more aware of what you have to be grateful for can help shift your mindset from one of misery to joy, from struggle to flow and from scarcity to abundance, leading to greater contentment and fulfilment in your life.

Take action in your workbook: Write down all the things you can think of now off the top of your head that you have to be grateful for. List all the things in your life that bring you joy and happiness, things you experience that make you feel proud, happy or lucky. This can be little things like the position of your house allowing for beautiful views of sunsets every day or big things like the roof over your head, the blood in your views sustaining life and everything else in-between (you know that's pretty essential for the whole "being alive" thing. Don't forget all the in-between things too. Maybe it's the way your morning coffee tastes like a hug in a mug, or the way your dog greets you like you've been gone for years when you've been gone for ten minutes dropping the kids at school. It could be that perfectly timed green light on your commute, or the satisfaction of peeling a sticker off in one go. Write it all down and watch your mood lift faster than a helium balloon at a kid's birthday party.

6. Breathe: (Not just the automatic kind of breathing keeping you alive)

There are a few different breathing techniques that work to regulate your heart and nervous system to bring calm to your mind and body and recentre you in overwhelming situations. One is the 4-7-8 technique which can calm your anxiety and stress. Breathe in through the nose for 4 seconds, hold for 7 seconds and exhale for 8 seconds. If you struggle to do that, inhaling for three seconds and out for 6 seconds can be beneficial too. Or you can do what is called a physiological sigh. This is a breathing technique the body naturally does to calm you from panic, hysterical crying or even when you're in deep sleep and there is a build-up of carbon dioxide in the bloodstream. For this technique you do two small inhales one after the other then a longer extended exhale. Typically, you do the double inhale through your nose and the exhale through your mouth but if for some reason you can't breathe through your nose or your mouth doing both breathes through either your nose or mouth is fine. This is a highly beneficial tool for calming your body when stressed and one to three of these breaths will bring the levels of stress down fast.

Intentional breathing is a technique that is so beneficial and yet I hear a lot of people say (my past-self included) it doesn't work for them and the reason for that is simple. They are either not doing it right or not practising it enough. Breathing techniques work on a biological level to slow your heart rate and regulate your nervous system. This is a scientific fact and a tool that will work if you do it right and practice it regularly. The trick here is to practice this breathing technique when you are feeling fine and dandy, so you get good at it. That way when you're in a stressful situation you don't have to think about what to do or how to do it, you already know how because you've practised it.

Working with kids with additional mental health needs and disabilities, one of the things we learn about de-escalating a heightened child is to not try to tell them to do something or explain how to do something in the heat of an emotional meltdown. This is because the thinking part of the brain is offline while the protective stress response part is in full flight. We are taught to teach kids de-escalation and calming strategies when they are in a good state of mind so they can better understand how to help themselves when getting overwhelmed. Adults are the same and a lot of us need it just as much as kids because we weren't taught this when we were young. Practice it while you're washing up, cooking dinner, cleaning the house, driving to work, walking the dog or any other time when you are already in a calm state of mind and soon, you'll find you automatically start doing it the moment you feel that bubbling bitch of overwhelm, upset or anger rumbling in your solar plexus in a challenging situation.

Once you get good at doing this and your mind and body feel calmer, you can channel your awareness to the present moment to understand what you are thinking and feeling and why, to redirect and re-program the script.

Take action: While this is not a step you can write about in your workbook, take action now by putting the book down/pressing pause and for the next five minutes at least, practice these breathing techniques and see how they make you feel. Do you feel more relaxed? More calm? Set a reminder on your phone for random times throughout the day you know you will be home and practice them again and again until you start thinking of doing it without reminders. At the sink washing dishes? Practice your breathing. Walking to the mailbox to throw out the junk mail that keeps accumulating? Practice your breathing. Doing some paperwork at the dock while sinking ships down the pipeline? (Insert giggle here if you catch my stench – I mean drift). Practise your breathing whenever and wherever you can and get good at it.

There are many other mindfulness techniques you can learn about and try. By doing a simple search online you can explore all the options available to you. You don't have to do a million different things to have a huge impact on your ability to become more self-aware of your thoughts and feelings in everyday life. For me, I do a quick 10-minute meditation in the morning, focusing on gratitude and intentions, then I do another longer meditation in the afternoon called non-sleep-deep-rest, I journal every night before bed, often taking time to reflect on what I'm thinking and feeling and find the physiological sigh technique extremely beneficial in every single moment I feel stress or irritated (busting that bubbling bitch down). By incorporating these practices into your daily life, you can develop greater self-awareness and cultivate a more positive and resilient mindset over time.

"Be content with what you have. Rejoice in how things are. When you realise there is nothing lacking the whole world belongs to you."

~ Lao Tzu

"Everything can be taken from a man but the last of the human freedoms – to choose one's attitudes in any given set of circumstances."

~ Viktor Frankl

"The difference between misery and happiness depends on what we do with our attention."

~ Sharon Salzbery

"Gratitude goes far beyond saying thank you. When we are grateful, we affirm that a source of goodness exists in our lives."

~ Robert A. Emmons

PART FIVE

Gratitude GPS: Finding joy in every direction

You have already come so far in the journey to transforming your mindset, setting yourself up for truly profound shifts in your life. While a lot of your focus so far has been on becoming aware of your past and present mindset and experiences, it's now time to train yourself to live and experience your life in joy and gratitude. We touched on this in the previous section but now we're going to dive deeper into developing the ability to be grateful. Psychologists say gratitude is essential in creating a positive mindset and learning how to live in joy and wholeness. Cultivating gratitude is how you reframe your thoughts to appreciate what you have and develop a positive outlook in any given moment or situation.

When you're living in stress and survival, focusing on lack, sadness, and struggle, it is so easy to forget all the amazing things in your life and the world around you. It's hard to focus on what you have to appreciate in life when your mind and body are programmed to feel and think negatively, attracted to the darkness, and seeped in a victim mentality. Even those of us who know we have a lot to be grateful for and are appreciative of the good in life, struggle to make this the predominant focus when life seems to be punching us in the guts over and over then kicking us while we're down.

Learning to appreciate the good, focusing on the amazing moments and living every day with gratitude and joy is essential to help shift our mindset and cultivate a life of wholeness, happiness, and abundance. When you've been struggling it's hard to think that is even possible and I know I didn't think I could. But it is possible even in the hardest situations. The trick is to establish an awareness and understanding of the difference between cultivating a positive, grateful mindset and practicing toxic positivity. When you get good at this, you start to see a lot of your struggle is perceived by the way you see yourself, your life, and the world around you as opposed to how things are and so much of your unhappiness can be shifted with intentional mindset changes.

I know that can seem hard to do when so many of us are not loaded in the bank account department, living in mansions, holidaying overseas in a new destination every season and running multi-million-dollar businesses. Life is hard because we grow up in minimum-wage families, living minimum-wage lives having to work all week for peanuts and pennies, experiencing struggle and trauma around every bend in the bumpy hill-ridden life path we're trekking along. We hear people talk about gratitude and wholeness, living an abundant life in happiness and think well that's easier said than done when time is always limited, work opportunities are limited, housing is an issue, the bills still need to be paid and life and price increases don't slow down just because we want to heal from our past and step into our best future.

But ordinary, everyday, people like us can achieve this amazing level of peace, joy, and wholeness; to live and feel abundant and happy every day. That is where your journey truly begins because when you start to learn how to do that, even when life is hard, you see something happen that is almost like magic. Your whole world shifts and suddenly it does not seem as hard or dark anymore. I know this because I made it happen in my everyday ordinary life with my bank account stripped bare from personal, financial and health crisis, clawing back from poor physical health, healing from a lifetime of depression, anxiety, and trauma with ADHD, three kids and a business depending on me and little to no support from others. So, I know you can do it too and you can do it with the information and advice I share through my work in this book and online.

Now, it's time to get your printout or book and brainstorm. We're going to look at how you can train your mind and body to see and feel the joy and gratitude of everyday life because that's where the real magic-like shifts start to happen. You have assessed your state of mind and identified your negative thoughts and behaviour patterns, focusing more on what you're lacking and struggling with so now it's time to turn it all around. Now it's time to put on your gratitude goggles and sprinkle some love confetti all over your chaotic, swirling shit-show of a life. Yep, right now. Because guess what? You can't wait for the dream job, dream house, or big payday and then feel like a wealthy rockstar. You can't just lose a few pounds, ditch the bad habits, or find your fairy tale love and then expect to magically become a beacon of confidence and happiness. But you can absolutely start right now, in the beautiful mess of your everyday life. So, let's dive into how to rock this gratitude party!

Step 1. As always, we start small with baby steps. Begin by incorporating intentional gratitude into your daily routine in manageable doses. Dedicate a few minutes each day, always in the morning and again before bed, to reflect on things you're thankful for and what is going well for you. Don't say "nothing" because there is always something and no matter how small or seemingly insignificant, every little win-moment is important. Begin your day by thinking about all the amazing things you will do and remind yourself what you are working towards, instead of focusing on your struggles and what has gone wrong in the past.

Starting your day off on the right foot is essential to cultivating an entire day of gratitude and helps set your mindset up to see the good instead of what's wrong. While there may be stressful or worrying issues that do require our time and attention to solve a problem or make a strategy for overcoming them, being aware of what you need to focus on and what is insignificant is essential. Then again at the end of the day, as you lie in bed don't ruminate on things that went wrong throughout the day or start stressing about upcoming worries, focus on everything that went well that day. Start running your day back over in your head and pick out every little win. Concentrate on these instances, telling yourself how grateful you are that you had these moments in your day and how excited you are for more possibilities for growth and success tomorrow.

For now, fill out the PDF (or write in your book) under 'Practicing Gratitude' step 1, listing at least three things you could focus on in the morning to elicit a sense of gratitude, and three things you could look for at the end of the day to focus on to appreciate the best parts of it. These could be things like:

- I could afford to put petrol in my car to get to work today.
- I am blessed to have a beautiful family to take care of and love.
- I am grateful to be fit enough to do a job that supports my family.
- While I didn't get the dishes done after dinner, I am so blessed to have the food to dirty those dishes for my family to eat.
- While our budget is tight and times are tough, it's amazing that I do so well to look after my family and myself to the best of my abilities.
- I'm excited to be growing and improving every day to be better for me and my loved ones.
- I am proud of my efforts, I acknowledge how far I've come despite my struggles, and I am grateful for the resilience to find the strength to keep focusing on the good even when times are tough.

Whatever it is in the context of your life, everyone, even in the toughest lives and situations has something to focus on to cultivate joy and gratitude. I know you can find these things too if you choose to focus on it. Now let's get to work figuring out what those things are and although we're starting small here, with time and practice your mindset will shift dramatically. Soon you will be living almost every moment of every day in joy and gratitude, and I promise it is the most amazing feeling in the world. Imagine that pang of love you get looking at your kids, the sunset, a dog's smile or whatever it is that makes you happy. Imagine having that feeling not just momentarily in special circumstances but most of the time and sometimes for barely any reason at all. It's an amazing way to live and no amount of money or success, no drink, no drug, and no other addiction even comes close.

Step 2. Start a gratitude journal to keep track of all the things you notice and feel that elicit your appreciation for your everyday life and surroundings. It doesn't have to be fancy or in-depth and if you're already journaling your thoughts and feelings, you don't need a separate gratitude journal, just add a bit at the end of each daily entry, listing the things you're grateful for. If you don't already do daily journaling, creating a "gratitude journal" can be as simple as having an exercise book or a Word doc with a date at the top of the page and bullet points listing those moments and aspects of your day you when felt grateful or found something to be joyful about. Honestly, this can take up only 5 or ten minutes of your day and that is time well spent if it means cultivating a stronger, more joyful mindset and most of us waste more time than that on social media or ruminating on negative thoughts anyway.

Writing down what you're grateful for can amplify its impact and most importantly, on the hard days when you feel like there wasn't a lot of good to focus on, you can go back over what you've written and be inspired to find moments you might not have realised were there, moments you might have completely overlooked if at the time you were focused on what was bringing you down. Even if you still only find a few things, seeing the record of all the other amazing moments you've been recognising and experiencing on other days, helps you to see the bigger picture.

You will always have tough moments and days when you feel off-kilter, especially in the beginning of shifting your mindset because you've been programmed to think, feel, and act a certain way for so long. That doesn't mean you are failing or incapable and having the journal helps you see just how much you are achieving and succeeding. So, start that right now. Go to the PDF workbook where there is a section to practice, open a Word document on your computer, or if you're using a book to record your activities from this guide, turn to the back of the book, flip it upside down like your teacher in class taught you to do and start working from the back (you can always grab another book next time you're out to dedicate to this if you want). Now think of all the things that have gone well for you so far today (and yesterday if it's still early in the day for you right now) and write them down.

Step 3. Verbally express gratitude for people and moments you experience throughout the day. Don't keep your gratitude to yourself but instead share it with others. This not only helps lift you and cultivate a habit of being grateful but brings joy and appreciation to others in your life too. Take the opportunity to express appreciation to friends, family, colleagues, and even strangers who have made a positive impact on your life. Whether through a heartfelt thank-you note or message, a kind gesture, or a simple verbal acknowledgment, expressing gratitude not only uplifts others but also strengthens your sense of connection and generosity.

Start now by thinking of someone who has had a big impact on your life or someone who helps you often. Maybe you know a person who might not directly help you but is always fun and uplifting to be around. Even if you feel like you don't have many people in your corner or have the cognitive distortion that no one likes you or appreciates you, I guarantee there are more people in your life to be grateful for than you realise (even if it's that random nameless clerk at the supermarket who always lights up the room when they're serving their customers). I always go 3 levels up when thanking clerks, reception people, or any stranger who helps me like "Thanks so much for being so bright and cheery while serving me, that really made my day" or "Keep up the good work, the world needs more upbeat energetic people like you behind the counter." Watch them light up when you do it and feel that sense of joy inside you at their glow.

Don't feel embarrassed or awkward about giving extra thanks for ordinary things or randomly reaching out to someone with a quick message that says something like: "Hi there, I hope you're well. I've been doing a bit of work lately on shifting my mindset to stop struggling and feel better in life and something I'm doing is learning to focus on the good things in my life. It made me think of you because you've always [insert reason such as been there for me, helped me at work, made me laugh, made me feel appreciated or accepted] and I wanted to let you know that I am grateful and appreciative of your [support, help, kindness etc]." This is a simple and amazing way to bring more gratitude and joy to your day and these tiny, easy moments can mean so much to the person you're acknowledging. Now, in your printout or book, write a quick list of people you can message or acknowledge and why and start sending out a random message every few days or so. Additionally, every time you interact with someone who does and says something helpful or kind, acknowledge it and show genuine thanks and appreciation for that person and their time.

Step 4. Like with everything mindset-related, you must constantly work to shift your perspective and train yourself to see challenges and setbacks through the lens of gratitude. It's often hard to feel grateful and joyous when things are going wrong but instead of looking at challenges as something holding us back or ruining our chances at success, cultivate a deep belief that everything happens as it should to move us in the direction we need to go. Challenges build resilience, and resilience is essential in cultivating true, intentional change in life. When things don't go as planned, remember that plans can change, directions can be altered, and mistakes can be the best teachers (kind of like that eccentric professor who forgets your name but gives the best life advice). Think of it this way: you've got the remote control to your life. Are you going to let stressful circumstances take the batteries out? No way! You're in charge. So, recognise that those challenges aren't your downfall – they're just plot twists in your epic story. Only you and your mindset can take the story to a happy ending. So, step up, open your mind and your heart, and start shifting your perspective. It's time to hit the mental "refresh" button and keep the narrative rolling in your favour!

Now, in your printout or book, write down three times/situations when you felt challenged or set back by events out of your control and reframe those moments to look at them in a new light. For example, if you lost a job or missed out on a business opportunity that you wanted, look at what things you've done since then that wouldn't be possible if you still had that job or what you might have missed out on had you taken on extra work with that job opportunity. Have you gone through a breakup with someone you thought you'd spend the rest of your life with? If they're no longer with you, then they weren't meant for you. This means you were likely experiencing situations in the relationship that didn't serve your best needs. Now, you're free to find what you truly want and need in your love life. If the relationship ended because you made mistakes or hurt the other person, take this as an opportunity to heal from the trauma or mental struggles that led to those actions. Don't hold onto guilt or regret. Use your mistakes and struggles as lessons to learn from and work towards becoming a better person. That's why we're here.

There is a lesson in every struggle and every mistake. There is something to take away from every negative moment of pain and suffering to shift in a way that shows a new perspective and a clearer vision of what you are meant to think and feel. By consistently integrating these gratitude practices into your life, you'll cultivate a profound sense of gratitude that permeates your thoughts, emotions, and actions, enriching your overall well-being and enhancing your relationships with others. You just need to take the time and have the patience to cultivate the ability to see the good in every moment.

It's hard at first, but as I noted before, eventually it becomes easier and automatic. Soon, your mindset and life transformation becomes akin to walking out of a dark, damp, cold room full of ghosts and bottomless pits of misery, through a doorway of light into warmth, magic and peaceful moments of joy and love. Sounds like fluff and stuff I know, and I was never one for all that, but it's the only way I can think to describe the amazing feeling of bliss I have every day, now that my mind and body are healed and loving life. That's what living in gratitude truly feels like to me.

"The human race is a monotonous affair. Most people spend the greatest part of their time working in order to live, and what little freedom remains so fills them with fear that they seek out any and every means to be rid of it."

~ Johann Wolfgang von Goethe

"Vulnerability is not knowing victory of defeat; it's understanding the necessity of both; it's engaging. It's being all in."

~ Brene Brown

"People often say that this or that person has not yet found himself. But the self is not something one finds; it is something one creates."

~ Thomas Szasz

PART SIX

Become Your Best Self: A journey to your 2.0 Version

You've heard the saying dress for the job you want, not the job you have, right? Well now that you have all the knowledge, tools, awareness and understanding about your mindset, how you want to change it and actions to take, you now have two very important steps to take. Firstly, you need to start thinking with the mindset you want, not the mindset you have and secondly, you need to behave in accordance with the positive attitudes you want to embody and act upon. If I told you at the beginning of all of this, if you want to have a positive mindset just think positive thoughts and eventually that's all you will think, you'd probably throw this book straight in the literal or virtual trash. Yeah, sure, just think happy thoughts and everything will all be ok. In hindsight, if you strip away all the work and complexities of a mindset reset, thinking positive thoughts is what it's all about on the surface level.

However, you can't just tell yourself to think happy thoughts without going deeper first and doing the inner work. Just thinking positive thoughts is toxic and unhelpful without understanding how and why you came to feel and act the way you do in your current life. It's also not going to serve you in any way if you don't first learn to understand yourself as an individual person and do the work to find out exactly what works for you. You can't think positive thoughts and not dig deeper and take action to behave in the way you need to change. That's like telling someone who has worked under the hood of a car before to just tell the car to run smoothly and get in it and go. Oh yeah that would work really well. How could you possibly get the car running smoothly without first learning about why it's clunking around under the hood in the first place, then understanding the work to fix it and of course actually doing said work to get it going. PLUS you don't always get it right the first time. Anyone who's had serious car problems knows sometimes you have to fix and replace more than one thing to finally get to the root of the problem and get that beasty purring right again.

Ok, I might of went on an analogy tangent just now but the main point is, to just think positive thoughts is not fixing an underlying problem. Trying to mask a problem with positive thoughts is what we call toxic positivity. "Thinking positively" and "having a positive mindset" are very different concepts. Someone who just thinks positive thoughts and tries to look on the bright side all the time and ignores the struggles and stressors will inevitably fall victim to the boiling, bubbling, growing mire of pain inside them. That stuff doesn't just go away with a sprinkle of positivity. Positivity isn't some bibbity-bobbitty fairy dust you thrust in the face of pain and struggle to make it vanish without a trace, no hard work and self-awareness needed (we wish it was that simple). Negative feelings aren't some dirty secret you need to lock away in a closet and toss the key in a deep river to be snacked upon by a kraken who will never return it to allow you back in to sort out your feelings. Negative feelings, traumatic experiences and detrimental habits need time, care and attention in the right way and dosage.

Most of all, a mindset shift requires action. You can change your thoughts and attitudes all you want but if you don't practice the behaviours associated with those thoughts and attitudes, you will stay stuck in your ways. Decades of study into social psychology suggests that a person's attitudes have little effect on their actual behaviour. In other words, a lot of people don't often practice what they preach and even if we have positive attitudes towards certain aspects of life (i.e. work, health, acceptance of others etc) if we don't take action that aligns with that, we will always behave in a manner contrary to what we think and believe. That's why this book is not just all about addressing the underlying issues behind your negative thought patterns, habits and limiting beliefs and ways you can reframe them and flip them, but about taking actual action in your everyday life to change the behaviours associated with these detrimental patterns. It's about identifying the negative thoughts and limiting beliefs that are complete lies or misconceptions based on external programming from your past and outer reality. That way you no longer feel tethered to these misconceptions and can start acting in a way that serves a better version of you and how you wish to behave in your life. It's about identifying issues with your life and mindset that can be changed and improved with conscious work and time.

One thing is for sure, no matter what limiting beliefs and negative patterns of thoughts you're working to rewire, you must continuously strive to be aware of them and make a conscious decision to act in a way that challenges them. Always reinforce your sense of worth and embody the qualities of the person you want to be. You may have heard the saying fake it until you make it right? That is NOT what I'm talking about here. When you say fake it until you make it, what you're doing is putting on a show on the surface while underneath thinking and feeling like you are not that person. Like you're just a fraud pretending to be someone you're not. Acting like the person you want to be is the concept of telling yourself you *are* this person who is calmer, organised, emotionally competent, happier, or whatever it is you want to embody. Henry Ford once said, "Whether you think you can or think you can't either way you're right." Our psychological wiring it programmed by us. We are the ones deciding who we are and what we feel based on our experiences, remember? The loop? Thoughts = feelings = actions = situations = thoughts and so on.

Be conscious about the thoughts arising in your day-to-day life and rather than acting how you normally would or making choices based on your past behaviours and habits, deliberately choose to act like the person you are working to become. Tell yourself, "I understand my past has programmed me to think and believe I am not [organised, fit, smart, patient, kind etc] but I am whoever I choose to be, and I choose to be [insert your goal trait]. This feels strange at first and your sneaky brain will try so hard to make you think the new way is a lie because it's so used to the comfort of the known, usual behaviours. However, with time, patience, and a whole lot of discipline from your conscious self, you will start to see dramatic shifts, I promise. By acting like the person you want to be, you're sending a clear message to yourself that you ARE the person you want to be, and this is an essential part of rewiring your internal programming.

Here's a hot tip. Something I've heard from countless people over and over that also aligns with how I used to feel, is that they just can't do this step because they can't believe it. You've really got to believe it to be true in order to make the shift work. This is a tricky thing to do. I'm not going to lie and tell you there's a magical hack and abracadabra you've been turned into the Prince or Princess of Whoop-Whoop. This is the reason why so many people stay stuck. Not believing in themselves. Everyone is different and everyone needs to find their own way eventually. Their own personal abracadabra. But here's an idea that worked for me and has worked for a lot of other people too. Get delusional. Yeah, you read that right. Get delusional. Pretend. Use the power of your imagination and make believe you are in your own screenplay of your life.

If you've ever delved into psychology, you may have come across a concept called 'the observer effect.' This concept denotes that people tend to behave differently when they know they are being observed. So, pretend you are on camera at all times, and you're tasked with acting out being the person you desperately want to be. What would a confident person do or how would they present themselves? How would a conscious parent interact and react with their children. Want to be a YouTuber but terrified of being on camera? Pretend you're on camera when you're not on camera and practice, practice, practice.

Why does this work? It's not just a fun idea but founded in psychology. Your brain doesn't know the difference between a thought about a situation or experiencing it in real life. That's why we feel sad, anxious, angry or happy when we think of memories that evoke those feelings. You're not going through the breakup right now but if it hurt then and you think about it now it hurts now just at the thought of it. You're not arguing with your nosy neighbour right this minute but if you think about the time they painted your dog pink and glued horns to your cat, you get fired up. The point is, the more you pretend and practice being a certain way or being in a certain situation, the more your brain starts to rewire itself. Eventually, the connections start to become real, not just pretend. But it is a slow process at first. You have to have the patience and understand that this will take time and be persistent enough in your real-time screenplay to keep going until your made up life-reel becomes real-life reality.

This seems crazy, I know. It seems absurd but here's the important thing to remember. You don't have to go around like the town-crazy shouting from the rooftops you're a billionaire rockstar with a yacht when that's obviously not true. This is a game you play privately in your head to start with, and you don't have to share this with anyone. This is about building confidence in your ability to be the person you want to be because contrary to what some people believe confidence is not something you're just born with.

Confidence is not the ability to just do something without caring or trying but the ability to try and to learn over and over. You don't get competent at something by being confident. You try, you learn, you fail, you try again and as you get better you start to gain CONFIDENCE. That is how it works and a lot of the time it starts in the background on your own without any big flashy signs showing off your progress and that's ok. So, when faced with a situation where you feel confidence is needed and that old you pipes up inside and says, "Oh I can't do that because I'm not confident enough," that is when you take action, and you act like the confident person you want to be. You shut that shit down and say, "I am a confident person because I am not afraid to fail. I will try my best at this and even if I fail miserably that is 100% better than letting opportunity pass me by," and then you just go for it.

Remember, even if you stuff up and fail you have still gained a lesson, more confidence, and a little bit of experience in what you're doing, but if you shy away in fear of failure and don't even try, you get nothing but regret and that awful, nagging feeling of what if. You might feel strange or silly "pretending" to be the person you want to be or playing make-believe games but is it worth it to completely change your life and the way you feel about yourself? Isn't a little silly delusional role-play a small price to pay to stop struggling and suffering with whatever it is you want to change? What is the better option? Failure and practice that gains experience, knowledge and a little extra confidence or avoidance that gives you regret, shame and the gut-eating hurt of never knowing what you might have gained from trying.

What if you're aiming for something a little more physical and hands-on like if you're trying to keep a less cluttered and more organised home? If this is something you struggle with, I highly recommend you start focusing on this as an area of improvement because clutter and disorganisation is stressful, and it hinders your mindset in profound ways. To focus on this, you might start aiming to tidy small amounts of mess and clutter each day. Remember pretend you are being watched. Pretend you're on a reality TV show called "Declutter My Life One Day at a Time," and commit to doing something every day no matter how small. Be more conscious when you're leaving things out that need to get put away. Neaten things sporadically when you see they're out of place and take the tiny steps to better your space whenever you can because that's what an organised person with a clutter-free house would do. If I've cleared out a space in my home and see a bargain cool shiny object at the store next week, do I get it just because I can and have a space for it now? No way. A person who is mindful of their space and actively trying to reduce clutter would not buy something to take up space unless it was a necessary item.

Even if you have ADHD and subconsciously leave things around, struggle with overwhelm and clutter and all the tricky stuff that comes with executive function issues (yes, I know how that goes because that is me), by working on your mind and doing tiny bite-sized bits, you can change and improve the way you function and live. The focus here is about 20% physical effort and 80% mental effort. What I mean is, if you have executive function issues from brain health conditions including ADHD, depression, anxiety, and trauma, you will struggle so much more to keep on top of things and that is okay. The way you approach your change and how you implement action to get on top of things will be different and that is also okay. The issue here is how we berate ourselves over it and expect we should do things a different way and it's not okay for you to do that because you're not doing anything wrong by doing things differently.

Just remember, with whatever you are working towards, everyone works differently and what works for one may not work for another. That's why instead of feeling like you SHOULD do something, acknowledge you are growing, learning, and trying and work with what you can do. Baby steps and small improvements are good enough and better than nothing. Part done in many cases, is good enough. Letting things lay around all day and having a 30-minute power clean in the evening is good enough. If you're working on battling your anxiety, going to the shops alone for ten minutes, even if you don't do a whole grocery shop, is good enough. If you're trying to get into a regular fitness routine, 5 minutes a day is good enough until you can work up to 10 then 15 then 20 and so on. But the more you do these things, all the while telling yourself you are this capable person who does these things regularly, the more imbedded, natural and automatic the desired behaviours become.

Your mindset around being who you want to be and doing what you need to achieve your goals is a bigger roadblock than anything else in your way. People think problems like time and money are holding them back but if you get to the bottom of things, time and money have a strong foundation in your mindset. The way you think and feel about money and how to make it. The way you think and feel about time and how much you have or don't have. When you get to the route of any issue that is stopping you from trying something or changing, your mindset is right there gripping the reins and trying to steer your destiny mischievously in the background, under the guise of all these other issues.

I know it is possible to change your entire life in profound ways simply by shifting the way you think about everything, acting in accordance with your goals and desires, taking tiny steps, eliciting small progress over time and being kind and patient with yourself along the way. To go from stress, chaos and rushing to calm, peace and time freedom. To go from overwhelm to relaxation. To go from depression to happiness. From anxiety to confidence. From struggling to living life in joy and best of all for me, going from an irritable, reactive parent to a calmer more intentional one who has seen dramatic shifts in their kids' emotional regulation because of it.

I have improved dramatically and completely changed my life in many areas that I previously struggled with so much and I did it all with the power of my mind, one little bit at a time. I didn't have a big support circle, a blessed life or lots of money. I wouldn't take medication for depression, anxiety, or ADHD (because the one time I was prescribed anti-depressants I didn't like how they made me feel so didn't continue taking them). I'm not saying that you shouldn't take medication if that's what is right for you (everyone should make their decisions based on their individual needs and professional advice, I am simply stating what I chose for me). All I'm saying is that if someone like me with a lifetime of struggles, trauma and unmedicated brain health issues can use the techniques I've shared with you to combat depression, anxiety, a negative mindset, parental struggles, self-loathing, clutter, disorganisation, poor time management and more, than that's a pretty good indicator of what is possible for others out there like me.

So now that you're ready to start being the person you want to be, I want you to pick one to three focus areas for the next three months to work on. It might not even take you three months to solidify these new habits and in that case, once one thing becomes easier and more automatic for you, then you start incorporating the next thing. The important thing here is to not take on too much at once. A lot of people make the mistake of getting impatient and wanting to change everything at once because they're so tired of the life they've been living for so long. That was my big mistake that I made over and over and even now sometimes the evil time distortion fairy pops up and tricks me into getting impatient with slower progress, the negative

Nellys niggle in the back of my mind whispering old detrimental thoughts. It will happen. Just notice when it does, flip your thinking and be gentle with yourself while you learn. Don't try to go on a diet, start a morning fitness routine, learn meditation and mindfulness, declutter your house and start work on that new project all at once. Give yourself a chance.

Pick one thing to focus on that will make the most impact in your life now and make that number one so even if you have one or two other things to focus on, keep the main one in sight first so you can drop the other two for now if you need to. Get your printout or book and write at the top of the page what your main focus for change is, then underneath list all the things you can think to do to help you shift that behaviour or thought pattern. It's also helpful to keep this one as an ongoing activity and as time goes on and you notice things you're struggling with in that area, you can add to the list the things you want to do or change.

For example, if your goal is to be a less reactive parent you might write some mantras to tell yourself when your patience is tested at common times. Maybe it's the morning or bedtime and you could aim to remember to do some breathing techniques to calm your nervous system and tell yourself "Being a little late for school is not as damaging as yelling at my child and causing emotional distress." Let's just get through the morning, be a little late and then work out what to change to help prevent this in the future. Whatever it is, recognise what is hindering the routine, take a breath and make a mental note of what you can do differently the next day. Then write that down in your journal to work on and tell yourself, we are struggling now but we will keep working towards doing better. We are trying and we will do better with time and practice.

You've got this; you really do. You are the person you want to be underneath all the struggle and pain; you just need to dig through that stuff to free yourself. You can be whoever you choose to be and act however you choose to act. When you were young, if you were lucky enough to have a parent, teacher or another adult in your life who believed in the endless possibilities of consistent effort and positive thinking, you may have had someone tell you, "Always try your best and work at what you love and you can be whatever you want to be." The concept of this still stands at any time in your life and while you might not become an astronaut or deep-sea diver or be limited from some other dream or profession for a true, valid reason, most of the possibilities are available to you. Most of your dreams and goals are there for the taking if you do the work, take the time, and have the patience to learn and grow and make changes where needed.

We are so blessed to live in an age of opportunities, technologies, and a wealth of knowledge at our fingertips to help us grow and succeed in a multitude of ways. The biggest thing holding you back from having the life you want is a bit of sneaky, intelligent mush inside your head that has fooled you into believing you don't have as much control over your life as you do. You *do* have control over your life, and you *do* have control over that sneaky little blob of mush. The sooner you realise that and start taking action to be the you you want to be, the sooner you can grow your wings and fly to the heights you so desperately crave to explore.

Final Words

Congratulations Mindset Reset Warrior; you made it to the end of the first book in our 90 Days to Success series and by now I know you're right on track with shifting your mindset in a way that will truly transform your life. By reading this book and committing to your transformative journey, you've taken the first and most significant step towards creating a more positive, resilient, and empowered mindset and living the life you dream of living. But your work is not done yet. The work is never done for superheroes like you and me because learning, growing, and evolving is a lifetime commitment and one worth the focus to live a joyful, whole life in happiness and abundance.

Always remember that cultivating a positive mindset is an ongoing process and continue to apply the techniques and strategies you've learned beyond the 90 days. These books are made to hold your focus on each transformation aspect for 90 days as that is the average time it takes to rewire your brain and create a new habit, or to solidify new learning and with the right action plan it's amazing what you can achieve in just 12 weeks. It might take less time and sometimes a little more to get the hang of some things (research says it takes anywhere from 1-6 months to solidify new habits). But what I can guarantee, based on scientific evidence and my own personal experience, is no matter how long it takes, with consistency, patience and repetition, the changes you're working on will happen and once you create a new habit and work on it long enough, your brain will automate it. The more positive things your brain automates, the more you shift from hindering thoughts to helpful thoughts, from detrimental habits and patterns to helpful and transformative action, and the easier life becomes. Once you get past the hard slog, life rapidly goes from struggle to flow like you wouldn't believe and that's what we're aiming for. Long-term success, not short-term band-aid fixes.

At first, it's a lot of hard work, a lot of rebuilding and a lot of discipline and determination but once things start to shift, suddenly all your goals and targets get easier and take less time. I've likened this to a snowball effect or a domino effect. It's truly an amazing feeling to experience this rapid shift when it starts to occur. As I said, at first it's hard, and so many life coaches and motivational speakers and the like will say change is easy if you just try this and that and it's all simpler than you think. So many will try to tell you there are hacks and tricks and simple easy steps to convince you they have some big secret figured out to get you to throw huge wads of your hard-earned money at them. The truth is, it is really challenging, and it takes time at first and that is why so many people give up. They've been fooled into thinking it should be easier so there must be something broken and unrepairable within them if they can't function the way society expects them to. That they're not capable or made for happiness and success if they've tried to change in the past and never made things work or stick. However, the more aspects of your life you change to serve you instead of struggle through, the more work, time, and patience you invest in yourself at the beginning, continuing to believe in your abilities and hold out for bigger, better things, knowing they are coming, the easier it all becomes in the long run.

To give you a visual of this, imagine you see a massive sack and it is chockers full of little rocks and on each rock is the name of a goal, habit, or trait you need to develop to live your best life. You know you need to master and carry all these things to get onto a path of happiness and wholeness but it's far too much to carry all at once when you're not yet strong enough to handle it. But you're tired of struggling and know this is what you need to make it in life. You're pumped. You're ready for change. You've watched the motivational videos and read the books and you're inspired to tackle all the things you need to tackle. You're charged and ready to move forward. You grab that sack, pick it up and start on your way. The sack is heavy, but you're all pumped up and powering through the strain of carrying it all at once. In the sack is positive mind shifts you're not used to, a fitness routine that your body hasn't eased into, a diet that takes a lot of memory and effort, a book, business idea or project that needs work every day if you're ever going to get it done and so many other things. It's heavy. It's complicated. It's too much and so you start to chuck some of those rocks out of the bag to make it easier and lighter to carry. You're dropping all the rocks and usually painfully onto your toes while telling yourself you're failing or useless or you just drop the whole bag altogether and go back to dragging your feet through life, thinking you're just not capable of carrying this stuff.

Now look beside you on your alternate life path and there is another version of you. They have an empty sack and on the road in front of them is a single rock with a single habit to master. The first rock is mindset. They pick it up and as they walk, they examine the rock, they hold it, get familiar with it, grow stronger from it, and then pop it in their sack before stopping to pick up the next rock. They do the same again and again until their sack is full of rocks with all the habits, traits, and goals they've accumulated and yet the sack is light as a feather because they started small, and their strength grew over time. If you walk into a gym and try to lift the heaviest weight without proper training you will struggle but if you start lighter and work your way up to it, by the time you reach the biggest weight the effort will be minimal, and you will barely notice the work it takes (because over time you've already done all the work in tiny bite-sized amounts).

This is what true transformation is all about. Taking time and having patience and faith in yourself to know that while right now it is hard and slow, eventually it will become easier and take less time and effort. That is worth waiting for. That is worth working towards because here's the kicker. You can do the hard work in a slow-paced manner for one year and by the next year, you will be feeling so much better, taking less time and effort to change and transform your life in profound ways. In five years, you're a completely different person with a beautiful outlook on life, the job you love, goals you've worked towards achieved with more in the works and a lifetime of possibilities ahead of you. OR you can give up. You can give into the lying, conniving voice in your head telling you it's not possible for you and it's too hard and takes too much time to do X,Y,Z and in one year you will feel the same or worse. You'll still be struggling and depressed. You'll still be wishing you'd done things differently yet still not taking the actions to change because you think you don't have the time, money, confidence, knowledge etc or it's too late, too hard, too scary, or not possible for you. In five years, you'll be the same or worse. In ten years, you'll be the same or worse and before you know it, you'll be taking your last breaths looking back at the life you could have changed but didn't and by then it *will* be too late.

There is only one "secret" here, the "hack", the "trick", or whatever you want to call it. Throughout your transformative journey you must shift your focus in the short term from the results to concentrate on the process and the execution of the process. That's not to say you don't think about the results at all because mental rehearsal entails you creating a picture in your mind of who you want to be and that is inspiration and motivation you need to get your blood pumping and your heart thumping, no doubt. But you don't focus on the fact you are *not* there yet. Too many people get caught up in the results and when they don't see big changes fast, they give up fast.

But the results don't always come quickly. Often, they come slowly over time but what you can concentrate on is the process and how you execute your goals, how you take action to make it happen and the million tiny steps you are taking in the right direction. When you focus on the process instead of the end results, even when there are not significant results you still can see progress because you see yourself taking action day after day. You see yourself starting to shift your habits and your focus, challenge those negative thoughts; you start feeling better a little bit at a time. You might not see the results now but if you are determined to make this work and keep taking repeated action in the right direction eventually you WILL look back and see how far you have come. I promise you that (and I don't make promises lightly – just ask my kids).

You can do this; I know you can. You can make profound changes in your life no matter who you are or where you're starting from. Don't let your brain tell you otherwise. Don't let anyone in this world or any situation brainwash you into thinking you can't be the person you want to be for any reason. At any point in time between now and that last breath, it is not too late for you if you choose it; if you embrace challenges as opportunities for growth, cultivate self-awareness and self-love, and nurture a mindset that supports your goals and aspirations no matter what. No matter your age, experiences, or circumstances you can change your life if you choose to start and you keep choosing every day to keep going, one little step towards change at a time. Don't take my word and my personal miraculous experience for it. Believe in decades and even centuries of research and information that tells you the mind is the gatekeeper to your life. From countless successful people throughout time who have shaped their lives on the power of their mindsets, all in different ways that worked for them personally (and not just intellectually intelligent people but anyone from any walk of life).

I know you can do this. I believe in you even if you don't. Let me be your cheerleader who will believe in your ability to change until you develop the strength and the capacity to believe in yourself. If you're struggling and want more help and advice, please check out my YouTube Channel, TikTok and Facebook for inspiration and reach out if you need a safe, judgement-free ear to listen. Also, be sure to keep your eyes peeled for the next book in the 90 Days to Success serries to keep learning how to shift your reality into a more purposeful and joyful existence. I hope you have enjoyed reading this book as much as I have enjoyed writing it to share with you and if so, please be sure to let me know your thoughts. Feedback is like crack to a writer, or chocolate, or air or whatever analogy is most appropriate. It's essential for improving and developing future content and works to share. So send me an email via the Mindset Warriors website, post a goofy pic of you reading my book on my social media pages, and leave an Amazon review. This also helps others find value in the content they are seeking to purchase and aids towards their decision whether this book is worth their while which I sure hope it is. May your journey of mindset reset bring you closer to living the fulfilling and purposeful life that you deserve.

Bye for now Mindset Reset Warriors. Peace, love, warm fuzzies and all that but most of all, take care. Of you! Because you're worth it.

Affirmations

The Fun & Spicy Ones

I am a mindset reset warrior & NO ONE can stop me but ME!

I am a magnet for awesomeness and attract epic vibes.

I slay my goals like a boss and look fabulous doing it.

I am the director and lead role of my own life, and I run this show.

I am too glam to give a damn about negativity.

I sprinkle kindness and sass wherever I go.

I am a fabulous work in progress, and that's perfectly fine.

I am a force of nature, unstoppable and undeniably amazing.

I radiate confidence and charm like a superstar.

I am a masterpiece in progress, and I love every brushstroke.

I am a unique blend of sparkle, strength, and spice.

I am a rock star at life, and my playlist is pure gold.

I am fabulous, fierce, and forever flourishing.

I am a walking, talking, dazzling success story.

I am the captain of my own ship, and I navigate with flair.

I am a delightful mix of wit, wisdom, and wonder.

Affirmations

The Light & Fluffy, Warm & Fuzzy Ones

I am the architect of my life and only I can control my destiny!

I am worthy of love, respect, and acceptance.

I embrace my strengths and honour my vulnerabilities.

I am capable of achieving my goals and dreams.

I trust the process of life and know that I am on the right path.

I release past hurts and embrace the present with an open heart.

I am resilient and can overcome any challenge.

I am grateful for the lessons that each experience brings.

I choose to focus on the positive aspects of my life.

I am deserving of happiness and fulfillment.

I nurture my mind, body, and spirit with loving care.

I am continuously growing and evolving into my best self.

I forgive myself and others, freeing myself from the past.

I trust in my inner wisdom and intuition.

I create my own reality through my thoughts and actions.

I am at peace with who I am and excited about who I am becoming.

Follow me on Social Media

www.facebook.com/mindsetresetwarriors

www.facebook.com/hlwaltonauthor

www.instagram.com/mindsetresetwarriors

www.instagram.com/helenwaltonauthor

www.tiktok.com/@mindsetresetwarriors

www.youtube.com/@mindsetresetwarriors

www.ingramcontent.com/pod-product-compliance
Lightning Source LLC
Chambersburg PA
CBHW071023250726
48653CB00005B/1688